CW00821144

GHOSTS
OF
ST. VINCENT'S

TOM EUBANKS

GHOSTS OF ST. VINCENT'S
Copyright © 2017 by Tom Eubanks. All rights reserved.
Published in the United States of America by TOMUS NYC.

Cover photograph by Tom Eubanks

LIBRARY OF CONGRESS CONTROL NUMBER 2017903177

ISBN: 0-69-284642-5
ISBN-13: 978-0-69-284642-1

TO MJH,

My Patience
& My Fortitude

In *The Last Puritan: A Memoir in the Form of a Novel,* George Santayana wrote, "Nothing is wholly historical, nothing is wholly imaginary." This serves as a good disclaimer for the following pages.

I would only add, no one is wholly fictional, no one is wholly real.

PROLOGUE: KING CHOLERA
(1849)

"Those sickened must be cured or die off, & being chiefly of the very scum of
the city, the quicker (their) dispatch the sooner the malady will cease."
—John Pintard,
Founder of the New York Historical Society
(regarding the 1832 cholera epidemic)

Sister Magdalena held Carrig's hand as the opium
suppository took effect. His eyelashes fluttered. He let
out a moan. Sister Magdalena could have sworn that he
had smiled. In the week that he had been under her care,
she had never seen anything resembling joy on the boy's
sunken face.

No one knew Carrig's exact age; they estimated he
was about eleven. They knew he was the latest of the
Buckleys to fall prey to the miasmas. Cholera took his
mother first, fresh off the ship. His father quickly

followed, felled by tuberculosis. Their eldest boy, Alroy, perished soon after, leaving Carrig in the hands of his older sisters, Mary and Margaret, who died in the Half Orphan Asylum, one after the other, hand-in-hand, in stained and stinking bedclothes. Their bodies were dumped like sacks of Irish Lumpers on Randall's Island. Sister Magdalena imagined that the rest of Carrig's family met the same fate. No one knew for sure. Only Carrig cared, but he was too busy fighting for his life in one of the 30 beds assembled in a small brick house named for Saint Vincent de Paul.

For those who knew their saints—and devout little Carrig, when coherent, prided himself on his knowledge of the patron saints—Saint Vincent de Paul dedicated his life to the indigent. Which is just what the lower wards of Manhattan needed when "the scourge of the poor" reared its deathly head again.

Her first year out of convent, Sister Magdalena tended to the sick during the last cholera epidemic seventeen years earlier. That was when, out of a population of 250,000, more than 3,500 New Yorkers perished.

Just outside of Lourdes, a fellow "grey sister" with whom Sister Magdalena corresponded wrote about the European headlines that crowned the pandemic, "King Cholera." A cruel, merciless monarch to be sure, the Sisters agreed. It claimed the lives of 100,000 French citizens in one year.

Although an ocean separated the Sisters, they shared the common experiences of desperate people surrounded by death while waiting for their own demise. Bodies oozing life in the foulest and most undignified fashion. Buckets of waste loaded onto mule-drawn wagons. Piles of mattresses, linens, and clothing, much of it children's, tossed into bonfires that cast demonic shadows on alley walls. Rows of rigid, decomposing bodies carted off to mass graves in the dead of night.

The Sisters of Charity could not bear to relive the nightmare of the last plague, so under the banner of St. Vincent, they took it upon themselves to provide a hospital to care for those who'd been given up for dead.

Unfortunately, the ignorance and discrimination that accompanied the last epidemic still ruled the day. Cholera victims were lepers without a colony, as they had been in 1832. There was still no cure, and no one was willing to take them in. Sure, there were more doctors than ever in the city, but many were quacks and most were expensive. People went mad or overdosed from tonics made of mercury and lead that were advertised in the penny presses and sold on street corners.

The Sisters found modest success treating cholera with a mix of sweat, sedation, and near-starvation. They combined the folk remedy of mustard, camphor, and cayenne pepper poultices to coax a sweat as the patient slept. For older patients, laudanum was most effective for relieving excruciating pain and assuring rest. For younger patients such as Carrig, opium suppositories were the best way to induce "healing sleep."

All patients were given fresh water from a stream in

Chelsea and fed small courses of mashed vegetables that the Sisters grew in their garden. Meat and alcohol were forbidden, and the noxious vapors from the swine-filled streets were kept at bay. Patients well enough to stand pressed their weary foreheads against sealed glass windows as the city bustled on.

It would be another five years before a London scientist confirmed what most traditional doctors had suspected. *Vibro cholerae* was transmitted through the wastewater of cholera victims. Contrary to the condemnation bandwagon overloaded with religious leaders and politicians, cholera was not a punishment for being poor. Nor was it divine retribution brought about by the blight of slavery, unfettered capitalism, Sabbath-breaking, infidelity, America's amoral war with Mexico, or any number of vices spreading through the country.

When President Taylor donned his star-spangled miter and urged the nation to repent before the epidemic reached biblical proportions and did to us what it did to the French in '32, Sister Magdalena was incensed. She allowed herself a smile of schadenfreude after the president died in office from cholera.

Carrig shuddered and hummed in his stuttering slumber as Sister Magdalena prayed. She vowed to God she would not let him go. His clan had escaped the Great Famine. They'd endured a trip across the Atlantic in steerage, only to be treated like pariahs when their packet ship docked. They had suffered and scraped and eventually succumbed. Sister Magdalena was determined

4

to uphold the family's dream by keeping Carrig alive.

"You will be my Lazarus," she whispered as she unfurled another blanket over the sleeping boy.

GHOST OF ST. VINCENT'S

"Night falls fast.
Today is in the past."

—Edna St. Vincent Millay,
Not So Far as the Forest

At the asphalt asterisk formed by the improbable intersection of 7th Avenue, Greenwich Avenue, and West 11th Street, workmen in DayGlo gear dismantle St. Vincent's Hospital. Ugly brown brick by ugly brown brick, they deconstruct the Brutalist '70s additions named for dead Catholic men: Coleman, Link, Cronin.

The red brick and limestone shells of the Smith and Raskob buildings along West 12th Street remain, sheathed in canary yellow scaffolding. Hollow windows resemble blackened eyes and broken teeth. The beige monolith in the middle of West 11th Street, named after Cardinal Francis Spellman, has been gutted.

Soon, all of it will be melded with re-barred chunks of pre-fabricated faux brick and tinted panes of glass to become "The Greenwich Lane."

According to *The New York Times*, prices at the condominium complex are expected to average $3,500 a square foot. Also featured: five townhouses with their own addresses, "as well as elevators, terraces and wood-fired pizza ovens." The "most affordable unit," a one-bedroom at 155 West 11th Street, will be listed for $2.05 million, with a tacit understanding that it will sell (and re-sell) for much more. It is a far cry from the "unique form of charity" the *Times* found here in 1892 when its reporter described "a crowd of persons in all stages of poverty and uncleanliness waiting for their turn to be admitted to a narrow hall in the basement [of St. Vincent's] to get a bowl of soup and a piece of bread."

"Its government is Roman Catholic," *The Irish-American Newspaper* announced when the Sisters of Charity opened the city's first Catholic hospital in the spring of 1849, "but persons of all religious denominations are admitted. For patients in the general ward—for board, washing, medical attendance, nursing, medicine, etc.—the charge will be $3 per week. As many patients as the means of the Institution permit, are received free."

When Cardinal Francis Spellman held a fund drive to enlarge the hospital in 1942, Mayor LaGuardia told the assembled: "St. Vincent's belongs to the people of this city, and even if there was no war, it would need to be larger, as it is located in a district where more and more people are going to live and big new apartment buildings are going up all the time."

Once a neighborhood of artists, writers, and revolutionaries, Greenwich Village has become one of the most expensive places to live in the world. LaGuardia would be appalled to hear that so-called luxury housing trumps hospitals.

I walk by the landmark's active ruins every day, past the earth-moving caterpillars, the 25-story crane, the temporary view of the Jefferson Market clock tower in the distance.

"Live *exactly* where you want," the signage crows, italicized entitlement compliments of the Rudin marketing team. A longer billboard stretches across the entire block, hovering where the hospital's 4th floor once existed and promising "a collection of *five unique addresses and five townhouses* nestled together in the West Village."

For 161 years, St. Vincent's treated immigrants, statesmen, poets, yuppies, punks, soldiers of the Civil War, survivors of the Titanic, artists of Bohemia, activists of Gay Rights, the shooting victims of Bernie Goetz, survivors of 9/11, and, in an uplifting farewell nod, the shaken passengers of US Airways Flight 1549 after their goose-downed Airbus A320 landed in the Hudson River.

Yet, despite numerous cameos in American history, St. Vincent's will be remembered most for its starring role in a modern plague. In 1981, the hospital reported one of the first diagnoses of Gay Related Immunodeficiency, or "GRID." Initially, GRID had been called "gay cancer."

Thanks to Haitians, heroin addicts, and hemophiliacs, the acronym "AIDS" (for "acquired immunodeficiency syndrome") replaced GRID, as it was more inclusive.

Although St. Vincent's was a conservative Catholic institution, its charitable history, its location in gay gay gay Greenwich Village, and its mission statement of "respect, integrity, compassion, and excellence" obligated the institution to transform its sprawling 7th floor into the city's first AIDS ward. In 1986, one third of St. Vincent's 758 beds were filled with AIDS patients.

On September 11, 2001, the trauma center at St. Vincent's treated more than 800 people after the destruction of the Twin Towers. Nurses who had served on the 7th floor were specifically recruited in the efforts because of their previous "war zone" experience. In the grim, sunny weeks that followed, desperate New Yorkers plastered the southern exterior of the hospital with Xeroxed wanted posters for the missing, an ephemeral shrine to the never-found.

In 1946, New York Governor Alfred E. Smith held his first eponymous dinner, a presidential political tradition to this day, to raise money to fund an expansion of St. Vincent's. It's therefore fitting that his great-great grandson Alfred E. Smith IV, as head of the hospital's board of directors, put his ancestor's pet project to sleep.

In 2005, St. Vincent's filed for bankruptcy for the first time. Five years later, after a drawn-out passion play— and under conditions suspicious enough to warrant investigation by the district attorney—the hospital's prime, block-long footprint was bestowed upon Rudin Management Company and Global Holdings.

I lived there twenty years ago. Up on the 7th floor. If you consider six arduous months, from Halloween, 1995, to just before Easter the following year, living.

Although I was baptized at St. Mary of the Annunciation and once aspired to become a priest as a confused fourth grader at St. Gilbert's, my time in St. Vincent's had nothing to do with religious principle. My poverty, the hospital's proximity, and a grim prognosis were the reasons I ended up there. The 7th floor accepted AIDS patients on Medicaid, regardless of what they felt about Catholic dogma. They had no interest in converting the sick to sainthood.

The summer before I was admitted, the hospital recorded its highest number of fatalities attributed to the epidemic. Nationwide, the death toll from AIDS was at 62,734. Realistically and statistically, I was not expected to survive. But I did. I'm not a ghost. If anything, the virus is. Thanks to a daily handful of pills the virus lurks undetectably in my lymph nodes. The hospital's transmogrification also haunts me, reviving memories once left—as many of us were—for dead.

Brought back from the brink by Big Pharma, we arose from our sick beds to rejoin the living. In less materialistic parts of the world, the dramatic turnaround brought about by anti-viral medications and the miraculous recoveries of those thrilled to be alive is called the "Lazarus Effect." In the West, we prefer to call it

"Lazarus Syndrome." Survival means scrapping grand memorial plans, tossing out premature obituaries, negating obsolete codicils, forging ahead with guilt and regrets and credit card debt slung around our necks.

I never thought I would live to see the hospital that kept me alive replaced by 200 condominiums and five townhouses for "slumming" celebrities, hedge fund bros, and the offspring of oligarchs.

Although a smattering of old-time Villagers rose up to fight the destruction of St. Vincent's, money always wins. Especially in Manhattan. The hospital became its own twisted Lazarus story, the kind that's been played out in neighborhoods across the city. Before the entitled lived here exclusively, the marginalized died in droves.

DEATHTRAP

"We are free to do anything, live anywhere, it doesn't matter.
We're completely free and that's the horror."
—Andrew Holleran,
Dancer from the Dance

On August 24, 1967, among the sweltering subdivisions, cornfields, and wetland preserves of north suburban Chicagoland, a discordant couple doing their damnedest to get by with two sons, ages 4 and 5, brought me, unplanned, into their fragile world. It was the tail end of the Summer of Love, the cusp of the Me Decade, the sweet spot of the Jet Age. Two years later, Stonewall would open the floodgates of human sexuality. In hindsight, it's clear I was on a collision course with AIDS.

"He's got fairies in his soul," is how my mother would defend my overwrought imagination and willowy ways. My older brothers took it upon themselves to make fuck-certain said fairies didn't work their way out into the open where our neighbors might see.

Around the age of three, I recall stripping my brother's defenseless G.I. Joe of his tiny fatigues. Joe wasn't anatomically correct, but genitalia didn't register in my scope of embryonic desires. I wanted to explore the masculine attributes of the doll's pliable body: bearded chin, broad shoulders, barrel chest, rippled stomach, round biceps, trunk-like legs.

I was well aware that my brothers sought visual excitement from satin-skinned lynxes with puckered mouths and orbs of flesh in magazines stashed in the basement. I was far more interested in the *Forum* section at the front of *Penthouse*, full of letters from "actual readers," including bi-curious adventures: a three-way gone gay, a new hookah shared with a buddy, a frat house pledge-painting party turned nude, sticky romp. Signed "Confused, But Willing" and "Still Lovin' the Chicks," the letters were vague on locational specifics ("I'm writing from a private, Midwestern college...") and often tested human logic (" ... next thing I knew he was deep inside of me!"). Whether or not the letters were true, reading them blew the lid off my understanding of what it meant to be gay.

I was also captivated by the stray box advertisements, usually in red ink and scattered among the classified ads at the back of *The Chicago Sun-Times*. Cinemas with French names featured cryptic titles: *The Athlete, Boys in the Sand, L.A. Plays Itself.* "XXX-rated, ALL MALE CASTS!" the ads shouted, titillating and terrifying me at the same time.

Before I started second grade, my mother divorced

my father to marry one of his best friends. In a whirlwind of fog and fury, I went from being the youngest of three to the youngest of eight, with two new stepsisters, three new stepbrothers, and the harsh realization that *The Brady Bunch* was bunk. On Sundays, after mass at St. Gilbert's, my father would use his court-appointed visitation to take my brothers and me to the movies.

Kids weren't a big demographic for Hollywood in the 1970s; while I lobbied for age-appropriate titles, *Escape from Witch Mountain*, *The Apple Dumpling Gang*, *The Shaggy D.A.*, my brothers would sway the vote toward more inappropriate, R-rated pictures—*Race with the Devil*, *Carrie*, *The Enforcer*. Impaired by heartache, booze, and the need to please, our dad obliged their desires.

At the age of nine, I could recite Cheech and Chong routines by heart. In 1977 alone, the year I turned 10, I witnessed a desperate Frenchwoman abort her baby in a bathtub in *The Other Side of Midnight*; a lonely woman's one-night stands turn violent in *Looking for Mr. Goodbar*; a hockey team brutalize opponents for ratings in *Slap Shot*; and a pair of violent, Vietnam veteran-seeks-vengeance flicks, *Rolling Thunder* and *The Farmer* ("He doesn't get mad. He gets even.").

In seventh grade, when the bloody *Alien* burst forth from John Hurt's chest, my dad had to carry me, limp and pale, to the lobby to wait out the remainder of the movie. I had just begun to overcome my fear of water, including the bathtub, after being rattled by *Jaws* four years earlier. I can't imagine what might have happened if

I'd been allowed to go downtown and see *L.A. Plays Itself.*

Sure, we were under 17, Dad reasoned, but we were red-blooded American boys accompanied by an adult. I never mentioned—outside of confession—that the movies we saw were almost always on the list of prohibited films in the Chicago Archdiocese's weekly *Catholic Reader.*

The year Reagan was inaugurated, MTV launched, and the first cases of what would turn out to be called AIDS were diagnosed, I was thrown to the wolves of public high school. My brothers had left for college, but Dad and I continued our Sunday movie routine.

In January 1982, we saw *Deathtrap.* Adapted from an Ira Levin Broadway hit, the movie starred Michael Caine, Christopher Reeve, and Dyan Cannon. It seemed like a harmless old-fashioned mystery. The poster had a Rubik's Cube motif. Dad had a thing for Dyan Cannon. We knew little else about it.

The first third of the movie established an engaging premise: a blocked, successful writer and his wife conspire to kill a young playwright and steal his new script. In one of the movie's many twists, director Sidney Lumet chose to have the characters played by Michael Caine and Christopher Reeve kiss, to signify their hidden love for one another. The booing and jeering that erupted from the audience at the Hawthorne Cinema stunned me. A woman behind us screamed bloody murder. A man across the aisle repeated, "Dis-gus-ting! Dis-GUS-ting!!" as he headed for the exit.

By that point in my life, I'd seen a lot of repulsive things on-screen: rapes, murders, dismemberments, beheadings, Laurence Olivier terrorizing Dustin Hoffman's molars in *Marathon Man*. The outrage and panic that greeted *Deathtrap*'s homosexual lip-lock seemed unwarranted. I couldn't bear to check my dad's reaction. I lowered my head and shrank into my seat. Deep down I knew I was condemned to desire the kiss of another man and certain to be greeted by a violent chorus of boos and jeers—even worse—if that desire was ever made public. The theater's full-throated scorn was something my grandmother only hinted at when I pointed out a blue satin jacket with white piping at the mall. "That jacket's made for faggots," she hissed as she pulled me away.

For self-preservation, I remained in the closet. I learned how to pass and did what was expected of me. I pretended to like girls. I took them to dances and bought them nosegays. Like my older brothers, I joined football, baseball, and wrestling. Unlike them, I was a failure at sports. I hid in plain sight by acting up in class and cracking jokes. I won first place in speech competitions. I joined a local improv troupe. I mc'ed homecoming games. Senior year, I was voted "class clown." Extroversion, I learned, deflects attention. Underneath, I was terrified of being discovered. I felt like a serial killer.

One lonely Saturday night in the family living room, a vision of hope burst forth from the cathode rays of our console tv as *20/20* correspondent Geraldo Rivera reported from the dance floor at Studio 54. Surrounded by sweaty, shirtless men dancing together under glittering lights, he may as well have been reporting live from Heaven.

Soon after, I discovered a copy of Andy Warhol's *Interview* and an *After Dark* magazine at Kroch's and Brentano's at the mall. Instantly, I abandoned my slapdash plans to join the priesthood—breaking my mother's heart in the process—and decided to escape to New York once I graduated high school,. When New York University's Acting Program held auditions in Chicago, I polished off the Mercutio death speech I learned in Mrs. Johnson's AP English class and memorized Wesley's first act monologue from Sam Shepard's *Curse of the Starving Class*. In May, I was accepted into the Circle in the Square acting program in NYU's Tisch School of the Arts.

That summer, I drove down to Chicago and wandered the streets of the neighborhood near Wrigley Field where "fags" were known to roam. Cruising came naturally to me; within hours of parking, I met a sexy older guy (all of 28) named Dale, a native Chicagoan with shoulder-length hair, Tarzan's body, and a stereotypically Polish surname. We went back to his apartment on Wellington, just off Lake Shore Drive. Until I left for NYU, I hung out with him and his friends a few days a week, and then headed back to the suburbs, usually past my curfew. I told my family I'd met a girl in Oak Park named Darlene. When I drove down to Chicago, I said I was visiting her. Nobody asked questions when her "brother" Dale called for me on the phone.

Like deadly tornadoes in distant states, AIDS and HIV (always capitalized, as if they should be followed by exclamation points) made the news from time to time. Religious and political leaders blew hardest at first. Amoral lifestyles lead to disease and death, they claimed. Gay men and intravenous drug users should be quarantined and left to die horribly—as God intended. Just when it seemed that the human immunodeficiency virus was another blight aimed at homosexuals, the plight of a teen-aged hemophiliac named Ryan White overtook the news. Diagnosed with the virus at 13, Ryan's fight to attend school in Kokomo, Indiana, put a wholesome— and terrifying—spin on the media's coverage of HIV, which is that "innocent" people could get it.

The deterioration and deaths of those who should have been my mentors happened far out of my sight. The meager chorus of early activists had not reached the John Hughes movie set in which I eeked out my final days of high school. AIDS jokes were big. Fashioned from fear, they replaced any meaningful discourse.

On September 17, 1985, three years after AIDS had been coined and two months after the highly public death of his Hollywood compatriot, Rock Hudson, President Reagan uttered the acronym publicly for the first time. During a press conference, a reporter asked if the president might support "a massive government research program against AIDS like the one President Nixon launched against cancer."

"I have been supporting it for more than four years now," Reagan answered. "It's been one of the top priorities with us, and over the last four years, and including what we have in the budget for '86, it will amount to over a half billion dollars that we have provided for research on AIDS in addition to what I'm sure the other medical groups are doing."

In a follow up, the reporter quoted a top scientist at the National Cancer Institute who stated that the administration's program and proposed funding increase were "not nearly enough" to combat "the epidemic that has struck fear into the Nation's health workers and even its schoolchildren."

The president shook his head like Katherine Hepburn in *On Golden Pond.* "I think with our budgetary constraints and all, it seems to me that $126 million in a single year for research has got to be something of a vital contribution."

Reagan's proposed 1986 budget requested $85.5 million for AIDS spending—smaller than the AIDS budget for the City of San Francisco. Despite this, the next reporter switched topics to an upcoming U.S.-Soviet summit.

Two years later, as Princess Diana hugged people with HIV to demonstrate they weren't a threat to the public, Reagan pressured the U.S. Public Health Service to add AIDS to their list of "dangerous and contagious diseases." The following month, the Senate unanimously passed the Helms Amendment, which banned HIV-positive foreigners from entering the country. Despite the struggles of an Indiana teenager, and the considerable star-power of the "people's princess," AIDS—and the fear of AIDS—metastasized.

I was too busy trying to get through high school to put much thought into the virus, the syndrome, or the burgeoning crisis until I met an acquaintance of Dale's named Peter, a neurotic Chicagoan who made a small fortune in Los Angeles and, like me, was headed to New York in the fall. He was the first abstinent gay man, and consequently, the bitchiest queen I'd ever met. We hit it off immediately in his suite at the Drake Hotel.

Peter seemed to have it all figured out even though I found his constant barrage of one-liners slightly desperate and his self-imposed seven-year break from sex highly suspect. It turned out he did accept blow jobs, mostly from what he called "straight boys," usually out-of-work, gay-for-pay actors. This he deemed safe. He was shocked that I knew so little about "safe sex." To Dale's dismay, he sat me down and made sure I knew what I was getting myself into. Did we always use condoms? Did either of us have cuts in our mouths? Did I realize I was moving to a city reeling from AIDS? Did I know how many were sick and dying? As a gay man with a healthy sexual appetite, did I realize I was practically volunteering for the front lines?

I must have looked like a deer in headlights. Peter turned to Dale as if I had left the room and said, "He's asking for it."

Between snorts of Hollywood coke, Peter laid out a litany of things I must do to avoid the virus. One of them was: "Never share a coke straw!" He opened a small silver box with four silver tubes in green velvet trenches.

"They've been sterilized," he said, as he offered them to us. We all went in for a line and came up talking. It was my first beautiful blur of a night: snorting, smoking, drinking, flirting, laughing until the clubs closed, a life I would seek once I moved to New York.

The next morning, Dale told me I didn't have to look up Peter when we were in New York if I didn't want to.

Shortly before I left home, my mother took me to lunch at a mall restaurant with a nostalgic garage theme. Booths were repurposed from the back seats of muscle cars. Road maps plastered the walls. Every remaining inch was littered with defunct gas pumps, stacks of bald tires, twisted bumpers, battered license plates, and the rusty signs of extinct oil companies.

I thought I might use the rare occasion of being alone with my mother to come out of the closet. Telling either of my fathers or any of my siblings was out of the question. My relationship with my stepfather was fractious at best, and he was far too intolerant to handle what I had to say. My real father might have been accepting of me, but I worried too much about his drinking to wonder how he felt about my sexual orientation.

On paper, my mother should have been sophisticated enough to handle it. She attended Northwestern

University in the '50s. She's well read and sophisticated. She taught speech and directed high school theater. She introduced me to *Auntie Mame* and *Great Expectations* on tv. On Wednesday nights in high school, I would bunker down on the floor in the bedroom that she and her husband rarely left, and we'd watch *Dynasty* with its big-shouldered harpies, camp dialogue, and gay prodigal son, Steven Carrington. I imagined she'd had a troubled male student come to her after drama class and confess his longing for the quarterback. That's how it happened in the movies. Besides, she was a Democrat.

I wanted to order Bloody Marys and tell her that Darlene was Dale and share all my new adventures downtown. I wanted her to know the joy I felt, the freedom I'd found. I wanted to confess the truth. I didn't want her to hear from someone in the checkout line at the Pic-n-Save that her youngest was a fag.

But she had other plans, launching into a rehearsed monologue about the perils her baby was certain to encounter once I got to New York City. She cared more about what other people thought than she did about my own safety. Her outlook and advice were about comporting myself properly in "the crazy city."

She never mentioned AIDS or drugs—she couldn't imagine I'd be caught up in such things. Mostly, she wanted to caution me not to change. "I just don't want you going and getting *squirrelly* on me," she concluded.

"I'm not going to go and get 'squirrelly' on you, Mom."

AWFUL WEIGHT
(1892)

"Ah, awful weight! Infinity
Pressed down upon the finite Me!
My anguished spirit, like a bird,
Beating against my lips I heard;
Yet lay the weight so close about
There was no room for it without.
And so beneath the weight lay I
And suffered death, but could not die."
—Edna St. Vincent Millay,
Renascence

No one has ever been accused of drinking too much in New Orleans. And nobody faults an over-served individual from setting down the bottle to rest his head a spell. In the case of stevedore Charlie Buzelle, however, a nap on a bed of cotton bales in the hold of the El Monte after an afternoon on Bourbon Street went beyond the boundaries of proper drunken behavior.

When Charlie awoke in total darkness, paralyzed and sick to his stomach, he was stone cold sober and frighteningly aware of his position, below the deck of a sailing ship, entombed in soft exports. He could move his fingers and toes, actions as useless as his muffled cries for help. The porous materials allowed him to breathe, but panic caused him to hyperventilate.

On its ten-day journey through the Gulf of Mexico up the Eastern seaboard to the West Side piers of Manhattan, the El Monte rocked back and forth. Charlie heard nothing but the churning of the rudder, the creaking of the hull, and seawater slapping the bilge. He knew he was hundreds of feet below the deckhouse, far from anyone who might save him. The thought of being buried alive was preposterous. He hadn't come all the way from Maine, travelled halfway around the globe, only to be extinguished by the excess of other people's wealth in the hull of the El Monte. He prayed to God. Oh, please, let this be a horrible dream.

His heart sped up. Someone's bound to find me, he thought. Red's sure to report that I've gone missing. That is, if Red made it back to the ship. As he lost consciousness again, Charlie cursed his irresponsible friend.

Mad visions whirled about like one of Edison's Kinetoscopes tied to the neck of a bald eagle soaring over Rockland, Maine. Charlie's body floated as if gravity had been annulled and the mounds of cotton above him had vanished.

Charlie saw himself as a child, walking with his good friend Otis along Tillson's Wharf. He swam in the ocean and rolled along the rocky beach. He climbed Mount Megunticook and inhaled the verdant hills.

His dear sister, Cora, sat in the living room and concentrated on her knitting. A litter of kittens mewed at her feet. A floral print covered her swollen belly, but beyond the fabric he could see deep below the skin to the fetus—pink, curled like a prawn. Cora had been desperate when she discovered her pregnancy. In a rambling, emotional outburst, she was convinced the baby would kill her. After a few hours of calming talk, Charlie convinced her otherwise.

Let me live to see that baby, Charlie repeated. God, let me live to see that baby.

A bright light appeared, blinding Charlie momentarily. When his vision came to, he saw the El Monte as a ghost ship below him, its passengers and contents visible. Surrounded by ocean and sky without horizon, Charlie was buoyed by hundreds of seabirds—albatrosses, gannets, frigatebirds, pelicans. He rose with the uplift of their wings. All his life he had desired this: to touch the spiritual side of nature. He resigned himself to his Fate.

Although newspapers around the country featured Charlie's tale with large font headlines, Cora was left in the dark. Henry, her patient husband, agreed with the doctor: hearing about Charlie's condition would only worry Cora and possibly harm her baby. So Cora's sister Clem kept her busy in the front room and any news-

25

carrying visitors at bay, as the two stitched baby clothes. For all Cora knew, Charlie would be back in Rockland in time for the birth just as he had promised.

On February 15, 1892, Cora intercepted a Western Union telegram at the front door. "CHARLES BUSSELL WELL ENOUGH TO LEAVE HOSPITAL," it read. Immediately, Cora fainted.

When she came to, she found herself in bed and nearly naked. Clem smiled and wiped her brow with a sponge. "You're going into labor, sweetheart," said Henry.

Ten hours later, as the bells pealed to celebrate George Washington's birthday, a smiling baby girl with a matted carrot-top came into the world. As the family gathered to admire the child, they handed Cora a newly arrived letter from Charlie that concluded, "It's hard to kill yours truly."

Clem told Cora it was a miracle. "Ten days at sea, pinned in the hull without food or water. He was dead when they found him, Cora, and they brought him back to life!"

"What is the name of the hospital?" asked Cora.

"St. Vincent's," answered Clem.

Vincent would be such a lovely name for a boy. She gazed at her little girl; she was the spitting image of Charlie when he was a baby.

"I'd like to call her Edna," Cora told her husband. "And her middle name will be St. Vincent."

Henry spoke his baby daughter's name aloud:

"Edna St. Vincent Millay."

Although it had a certain poetry to it, he thought it mighty queer. He grunted his approval. Who was he to argue with miracles?

PELIGROSA PIERS

"Little did we dream, nights at the Saint, when sweat was licked off
dancers' bodies and kisses were exchanged, that years later
we would refuse to drink from the water fountain there."

—Andrew Holleran,
Snobs at Sea

"This ain't no party, this ain't no disco.
This ain't no foolin' around
No time for dancing, or lovey dovey
We ain't got time for that now."

—David Byrne,
Life During Wartime

On Monday, Wednesday, and Friday mornings I took
the A-train from West 4th Street to the Port Authority Bus
Terminal and into a neighborhood that reeked of diesel
fumes, burnt chestnuts, and hot dog water. Theater
gypsies, sex workers, and drug addicts added their own
blend of stale sweat, cheap colognes, and all manners of
smoke to the olfactory ambience.

In a couple of rickety walk-ups on 42nd Street a few desolate blocks east of the river, I attended classes in movement, improv, vocal work, monologues, and scene study.

Between classes I'd cluster with my cohorts on the sidewalk before the Samuel French Bookstore, memorizing monologues, rehearsing scenes, smoking cigarettes. When I was a kid I begged my parents to quit smoking, yet I took up Marlboro Reds as soon as I was on my own. All of us actors smoked: it deepened our voices, made us feel older, and saved us money we would have wasted on food. I expected to find many like-minded peers, but I only met one or two guys willing to come out.

The message was unmistakable in the autumn of 1985: come out and kiss your career goodbye. Sure, there were rumors and open secrets, assigned beards and denied assignations, but not one successful movie star or well-known tv actor was "openly gay." Even though mass media was inundated with gay men and lesbians, the stereotypes of fags as freaks and fools—fun, perhaps, but fatally flawed—persisted. The epidemic stigmatized us further.

In March 1986, *The New York Times* turned up the hysteria with William F. Buckley's infamous "Identify All Carriers" op-ed piece.

"Everyone detected with AIDS should be tattooed," Buckley wrote, "in the upper forearm to protect common needle users, and on the buttocks to prevent the victimization of other homosexuals."

To the general public, we were seen as diseased hosts looking to infect others. Whether we were infected or not was never questioned. The atmosphere served to rust the hinges and jam the closet doors gay activists had fought so hard to bust open the previous decades.

Although I hung out with a talented group of actors and filmmakers at NYU, I continued the Darlene charade with my long-distance relationship with Dale. One of my best girlfriends from high school gave me a framed glamour shot that I placed prominently in my dorm room. I told people it was Darlene back home.

Meanwhile, Dale's frenemy, Peter, moved to the city from L.A., as he said he would when we met in Chicago. He rented a one-bedroom in a spanking-new high-rise above the Tower Records across from Lincoln Center. Much different than the tiny, ground-floor dorm room on Washington Square South that I shared with a high school wrestling star from New Jersey and a kid from Staten Island who played bass in a punk band. Peter would call the dorm payphone and ask me to join him for a Broadway show, a dinner I could never afford, or to watch him spend thousands on black clothes at Charivari.

One night in October he took me to the famed gay haunt, The Saint, on 2nd Avenue, for the first—and last—time. It was nothing like legend claimed. Music pumped aggressively, festive lights soared across the psychedelic planetarium dome high above the main dance floor, but the crowd was sparse. The Adonises that once lured men to heartbreak were long gone, their dour spirits hung about, casting shadows of melancholy. The bleacher seat orgies were replaced by people sitting alone with their cigarettes. A smattering of gawkers, like me, shook our heads with disappointment.

Despite multiple bumps of Peter's pharmaceutical-grade cocaine, we could not get into the spirit of decadence the place had once been known for. Uptown, Studio 54 was also a shell of its former self. I'd arrived too late for the Dionysian fantasies Geraldo Rivera and Andy Warhol enticed me with.

On one hand, Manhattan was home to, and a way station for, the most beautiful men in the world where you could fall in love at every stoplight. Reciprocation, on the other hand, was a different story. Cruising the streets for pick-ups became an anthropological relic of the '70s as AIDS progressed. Gay men coupled up and left town. Others gave up sex—safe or otherwise—entirely. Many hit the gym, added steroids, labored for the Schwarzenegger look to prove how healthy they were.

The remaining gay bars, like their clientele, dwindled. The Upper West Side held a couple of neighborhood dives. The Upper East Side was known for "checkbook" bars where younger men were propositioned by older men singing "I'd Rather Be Blue Over You" around a grand piano. Scattered around pre-Disney Times Square, the last of the city's famed peep shows and homoerotic cinemas crumbled. In desolate Chelsea, a video bar called Private Eyes pulled in a sweater-and-Cosmo crowd, including Peter and his guppie friends. The more established West Village scene featured Uncle Charlie's on Greenwich Avenue, a number of shady establishments along Christopher Street, historic Julius's on West 10th Street, and stalwart leather bars, the Spike and the Eagle's Nest, further north along the West Side Highway.

A younger, more androgynous demimonde blossomed in the East Village. Both the deliberately lower case boy bar, on St. Mark's Place, and the Pyramid Club, on Avenue A, promoted the neighborhood's twisted post-punk drag scene. Their uglier stepbrothers, The Boiler Room and The Tunnel Bar, served up draft beer, pool tables, and excellent jukeboxes. The far west side still had notorious sex clubs: Jay's, The Locker Room, Hellfire, The Anvil; the east side had a couple of frisky cinemas and some X-rated video stores with unmonitored buddy booths.

By 1987, the city's infamous bathhouses had been shuttered by the health department. Patrons, they said, were engaging in "high-risk sexual activities." The idea of men in towels prowling labyrinthine hallways in crowded saunas took root in my imagination in 1976 when my dad took my brothers and me to see *The Ritz*, a gay bathhouse farce starring Rita Moreno, Jack Weston, and a young Treat Williams. Yet another movie we did not consult Ebert and Siskel about before attending.

I resumed the process of coming out in earnest my sophomore year. After my college friends had retired for the night, I would wander the tree-lined streets of the

West Village, desultory old cow paths with Anglo names: Bank, Bleecker, Barrow, Bedford. On the sidewalks, I'd stumble across piles of books and magazines with familiar titles, outdated men's clothing, torn camp posters, random objects in black plastic bags: the effluvia that families from the provinces would not be taking home once they buried their sons.

The notorious shenanigans that once took place along the Hudson had been stunted by the time of my arrival, but hustlers and hookers still plied the patchwork of crumbling concrete. Johns parked perpendicular to the riverfront in campers and vans. Across from Christopher Street, transgendered runaways vogued along discarded railroad ties. Bull dykes and butch queens cheered them on from beyond the overgrown bushes. Brave late-night joggers navigated the obstacle course of discarded condoms on the asphalt expanse between the river and the highway. To the south, the World Trade Center towers, so drab in the daytime, twinkled.

Chain-link fencing, laced with hand-clipped holes for easy access, held signs that shouted, "PELIGROSA!" A family of squatters made a home on one of the more derelict piers that jutted out into the Hudson. Junkies, stoners, insomniacs, the curious and the desperate assembled in small cliques on the other piers. I considered my evening meanderings as anthropological investigations. For a young voyeur, the Hudson piers at night were pay dirt.

One night, crossing the West Side Highway, I noticed

a glimmering black BMW stopped at the light. In the back seat, through an open window, I noticed a familiar face gazing at the sunset. His steep pompadour, dark glasses, and black suit sharply contrasted the smooth, translucent skin stretched like pearly silk across his angular face. Of course I knew who it was. Not personally, but intimately. His name was on the waistband of my underwear. Universally known, richer than any human needed to be, he looked like the saddest vampire in the world.

Rumors about his health whirled during the epidemic, especially as his department store comrades—Perry Ellis, Willie Smith, Halston, Patrick Kelly—fell. Some said he underwent experimental treatments in Europe in which his blood was extracted, heated up, and pumped back into his body. Others claimed he received blood transfusions three times a day from healthy young donors.

The first time I saw him, during one of my clandestine upper-shelf magazine browses at Kroch's and Brentano's, I was around 15. In what I recall as a Spring issue of *GQ*, he appeared in a four-page spread focused on his work-out. In step-by-step photographs, the designer and his impossibly handsome trainer worked out on a Manhattan rooftop, surrounded by lush greenery and a postcard skyline view. It was the kind of life a young fag like me desperately sought.

My sophomore year, I found a part-time job at World of Video, a subterranean VHS rental place on Greenwich Avenue in the shadow of St. Vincent's

Hospital, a few doors down from the last of the West Village cruise bars, Uncle Charlie's.

After work one evening and a few margaritas at Banditos across the street, I gathered enough courage to go in to Uncle Charlie's. Sweater queens and neo-clones were in full happy hour cruise, standing in the swollen beams of light cast from the ceiling. Giant floral arrangements adorned each end of the long wooden bar. The hunky bartenders wore threadbare t-shirts and forced smiles. Music videos and Elaine Boosler stand-up routines played on wall-sized screens.

I bought a Rolling Rock and found a dark corner. As I sipped my beer, a tall, handsome guy with shoulder-length hair, a surfing t-shirt, and a big, easy smile approached me.

"Hi," he said, as if we'd met before. "You need a beer?"

I held up my bottle, two thirds full. It trembled in my hand. "I'm good. Thanks."

"I'm Ken." He held out his hand.

I grabbed it. We shook. I was glad to be drunk.

He asked if he'd seen me around the NYU gym, the Coles Sports Center on Mercer Street. I went there from time to time, but not as much as my roommate, the ex-wrestler from Jersey.

"You don't mean Josh, do you?" His face lit up. "I lift with Josh every now and then."

"I'm sure you do."

"He's straight."

"That's what I've gathered."

"But he sure is sexy."

"I suppose he is. He's not my type."

"Oh? What *is* your type?"

We left together that evening. He had a studio uptown but attended law school downtown, so he sublet a small one-bedroom near the West Side Highway so he could be closer to classes. The next day, I returned and waited outside his apartment to surprise him with a bouquet of flowers. As he approached the door, he broke down in tears. His doctor had just told him that he was HIV-positive. He was the first person I knew personally who had the diagnosis. We had just met and here he was, sentenced to death.

Beneath his worked-out 6-foot 2-inch frame and manipulative grin, Ken was a frayed ball of awkward. He had two other gay siblings, a brother and a sister, but as the oldest, their father judged him more harshly. Ken wanted to act as gaily as he felt, but his father's shame kept him in heteronormative check. The result was a handsome, tortured man, alternately stunning and stunted. What he lacked in social graces he more than made up for in heart. For my 19th birthday, he brought me to Fire Island and introduced me to that decadent strip of dunes and million-dollar shacks known as the Pines where we spent a magical week at the house of his best friends, Bobby and Stewart.

Bobby and Stewart lived like a pair of Uncle Mames. They were charter members of the pre-AIDS gay nexus of the West Village, the Pines, and Studio 54. Trips to Mykonos, Aruba, and Puerto Rico were sprinkled healthily into the schedule.

Of all the older queens I'd met as I navigated my coming out, Bobby was the only one who didn't ogle, condescend, or dismiss my presence altogether. He assumed the role of mentor and befriended me as an equal. He loaned me back issues of *Christopher Street* and *Drummer*. When I admitted to never having read *Dancer from the Dance*, he handed me the copy from his bookshelf. Above the REEEEEEEEE of the Osterizer in the sunny, second-floor kitchen on Neptune, he taught me how to make the perfect frozen margarita. Then he sat me down and asked me what I knew about AIDS.

I told him that AIDS and I were peers, how it arrived, alongside Madonna and MTV, just in time for my freshman year in 1981 at Warren Township High School. The summer I began to poke my nose out the closet, the world was already reeling from its dire impact. I never knew sex without the word "safe" attached to it like a poison label. I told him what Peter, still practicing his own version of abstinence, had said to me back at the Drake Hotel in Chicago. Aside from Ken, I didn't know anyone who had it.

"You're very lucky," Bobby said. "It's devastating to watch a young man's body and mind break down. It's different each time, but just as devastating."

I assured Bobby that I knew the consequences of "unsafe sex." Sheepishly, I admitted that I resented not having the freedom he and his friends had without someone sitting me down to talk about the importance of water-based lubricants and latex condoms.

"Even when you're giving head," he added with a shrug.

At the time, Bobby read everything concerning what we knew about AIDS and the human immunodeficiency virus just identified in laboratories. For the previous five years, he and Stewart had been on the front lines, unaware of what was coming at them. Friends and associates dropped without warning. Others showed up at parties with giveaway signs. They feared they might be next. Stewart was.

"Five years ago this weekend, God I'll never forget," Bobby marveled. "We got off the ferry—Darrell, dead last month, was visiting from Los Angeles—and right there in front of us, next to the Pavilion: a card table, a donation jar, and loud-mouthed Larry Kramer with a banner: 'Give to Gay Cancer.' And Darrell shouted, 'Don't you mean, Give to *Fight* Gay Cancer? Or are you for it?'"

We laughed because we were drunk. But later that night it dawned on me: this shit's here to stay. Multiple Sclerosis, Muscular Dystrophy, fucking Cat Leukemia— all the excuses we came up with to throw charity parties, to get fucked up and dance all night—have now been superseded. We've become the cause. The new banner on the dock of the Pines was named for us. Gay Cancer. Just lying in wait. We were so naïve.

After dinner on my birthday, Bobby and Stewart asked their bearded houseboy to doll himself up in his best San Francisco drag and lip-synch Gwen Guthrie's *Ain't Nothin' Goin' On But the Rent* before presenting me with a cake with flaming penis candles.

Bobby gave me the book he'd been reading that weekend, Tama Janowitz's *Slaves of New York*. The title page was filled with sexual innuendo and signatures from the weekend's houseguests.

Bobby's friendship was the best part of my doomed relationship with Ken. We went through a trying year. We had some physical altercations. I knew it had to end. I was entering midterms and behind on my schoolwork. I knew I'd be better off without the extra pressure. As if I could control life's pressures. Ken begged me to stay. I tried to resist, but his manic hypochondriasis and playing of the AIDS card wore me down.

That February, my father's profligate drinking and cigarette smoking came to an abrupt end. Sepsis seeped through his bloodstream, disabling organs on its indiscriminate march. I flew back to see him in the hospital, flat on his back, in a flimsy hospital gown, tubes shooting from the crook of his elbow, a respirator mask cupped to his face. He couldn't speak. With effort, he could muster a smile. His condition looked eerily reminiscent of an AIDS patient.

His blue eyes fixed on me in a purposeful stare. I like to think he was telling me that he knew about me, that it meant nothing to him, that he loved me regardless of who I was or who I slept with, that he wanted me to be happy, to find love, to live my life.

I'll never know what that final stare meant.

THE DIRECTOR & THE HEIRESS
(1963)

"...we'd go to Pearl's Chinese restaurant for supper. The first time we went
there, we opened our fortune cookies; his read, "Rise, take up thy bed and
walk" (he had just separated from Rita Gam), and mine, "You have met love
and all is well" (what signs and portents of the feelings exploding inside us.)"
— Gloria Vanderbilt,
on her relationship with Sidney Lumet

"It was only seven vodkas, a Miltown and idiocy."
— Sidney Lumet,
on the end of their marriage

Some blamed it on a seven-year itch, but Sid and Glo
knew it was more than that. Having achieved professional
successes on their own, the couple found themselves in
need of extracurricular scratching since their sudden
marriage in 1956. Since that time, he had been nominated
for awards and beckoned by Hollywood. She was
showing her paintings to great acclaim, and New York
City would always remain her home.

There was also the mutual matter of their fickle hearts. She had given hers to another man, a blue-eyed writer from Mississippi who made her feel alive again. He had allowed his to become familiar with another woman, another kind of heiress, the elegant daughter of Lena Horne.

The arrival of divorce papers came as no surprise to Sid—it was his second marriage, her third—but Glo's timing caught him off-guard. We have much greater things in our future if we part amicably, Glo assured him over the phone.

Fresh off his success with *Twelve Angry Men*, Sid rushed back to New York to salvage what he could of their wilting union. When he arrived at the penthouse, Glo was gone. She left a note, saying it was best they not see each other. Later, she phoned from the island to say that someone would be by to fix the hot water heater and since the help was on vacation, could he make sure he was around to let them in?

So that's it?

Haven't we said all we can say to one another as husband and wife? Might we get through this as adults and carry on as friends? What do you say, Sid?

What do I say? You expect me to have my death scene monologue prepared?

Do you need to be so over-dramatic?

As usual, they had resorted to tossing darted questions at each other without providing or expecting answers. Once they hung up, Sid grabbed a bottle of

Smirnoff and poured. Glo returned to her easel for a sunny afternoon of live model study in the garden. Her blue-eyed writer from the South was expected later for a swim.

Oppressively hot and humid, it seemed to Sid that an air conditioner repairman was needed more than the hot water guy. His restlessness, fueled by his fourth, fifth? Martini, turned into anger. He convinced himself that his wife was playing him for a schmuck. Asking him to wait around in the sweltering heat for the hot water guy. She knew the place was uninhabitable. Just like her ancestors, he thought, shuffling off to their country homes while the undesirables endure the piss-stinking, rat-filled glass and concrete oven of Manhattan.

Oven, he thought, walking to the library. He took his cocktail with him. On top of her reading table, alongside a well-thumbed galley of *The Feminine Mystique*, he spotted *The Colossus and Other Poems*. He picked the book up and began to read aloud as if he was his father on the stage of the Yiddish theater. He took swigs between poems until his glass was empty. He sat back in a chair and wept. His head swayed like a leaf in a gentle wind. He recalled the only time his wife had expressed the kind of emotion he now felt.

For all the years they had been together, he never really knew his wife. She refused to let him in. He thought he could get her to open up emotionally, as if she was one of his actresses, but her wall was too thick to penetrate, its surface too slick to climb. She could be joyous and generous and gay, but anything that veered too closely to the misery and sadness of her childhood was put on ice and locked away. The only time he had seen her break down was in February of that year, after she heard the news of Sylvia Plath's death. Since that time, she'd spent many hours rereading the poems he held in his unsteady hand.

He opened the book again and read. The words wormed off the pages. If this is what gets her attention, he thought. He made his way upstairs and opened the bathroom cabinet. Among the prescription bottles, he grabbed the one marked "Miltown" and returned downstairs.

He searched the bar for another bottle of vermouth. He switched on the radio. The Four Seasons sang "Walk Like a Man." Sneering in his stupor, Sid stirred his drink. He tossed a pill back and chased it with a sip of his Martini.

After 20 minutes of oldies, he began to feel the effects of the meprobamate on top of a bottle of Smirnoff. He felt the need to throw up but couldn't make it to the toilet. In desperate pain, touching the hem of mortality, he saw his situation a bit more clearly. I can't die like this. Over her. A footnote in her autobiography. My last act cannot be like something out of a B-movie.

As the weight of his eyelids proclaimed victory, Lesley Gore wailed, "It's my party and I'll cry if I want to ..." With all the strength he could muster, the director made his way down the elevator and to the street. He hailed a cab and shouted to the driver the first address that came to mind.

When he came to, he found himself in a bed at St. Vincent's. His throat felt raw; his stomach throbbed. He was hooked to an i.v. drip, and restraints held his arms and legs. Before him stood a vision: raven-haired, caramel-eyed, with a smile that lit up the dreary, semi-private room.

Sid thought nothing of his pumped stomach, or of Glo. Even the leather straps around his wrists and ankles meant nothing as he gazed into the eyes of the woman who would become his future wife, with whom he would have two beautiful daughters, a woman who would remain at his side for the next fifteen years as he directed some of the most important movies in the Hollywood canon.

"Looks like we got you here just in time, Lazarus," she said, a look of relief betraying her show of nonchalance. "It must have been an angel that dropped you in front of my door. I suppose it was a Checker? You don't remember, do you?"

He didn't. All he knew was that he'd never felt more grateful.

OUTLAW PARTY

"Repudiating the virtues of your world, criminals hopelessly
agree to organize a forbidden universe. They agree to live in it.
The air is nauseating: they can breathe it. But—criminals are remote from
you—as in love, they turn away from the world and its laws."

—Jean Genet,
The Thieves' Journal

I had every intention of coming out to my father. At 33,000 feet, while chain-smoking Marlboro Reds and knocking back mini bottles of Cuervo, I felt I had worked up enough courage to tell him that I was queer. When my brother picked me up at O'Hare, he asked if I'd like to get a drink before we went to the hospital. I thought nothing of it as we drove down the amber-lit expressway to the sounds of classic rock. Over a painfully sweet Ruby Tuesday's Margarita, he told me our dad succumbed to sepsis about an hour before my plane landed.

After the funeral, before I headed back to New York,

I took my mom aside and said, "I'm gay."

A sting of shame flashed across her face as if she'd been slapped. I could see it in her eyes: I had gone and gotten squirrelly. After she had specifically warned me not to. She cocked her head to one side: come again?

I hated the word, "gay." It didn't sound serious. It reeked of slander. My whole life it was the ultimate put-down. "Homosexual" was clinical-sounding and outdated; "gay" was a Molotov cocktail in our culture wars, tossed in with God and guns during election time, twisted and tainted for religious and political points. I could see my mom struggling. I wish there were a better word.

My mother prided herself on her Pollyanna outlook: to make a harsh world less so, smile and deny. It was an attitude that worked for her but didn't comport with my Harvey Milk meets Glenda philosophy ("come out, come out, wherever you are").

My mom and I had always been close, with similar interests and temperaments. I was a theatrical kid, easily anxious. She was a fellow neurotic haunted by a long-abandoned ambition to be Diane Sawyer. Societal expectations of marriage and family pressured her to pursue teaching instead. She read voraciously. I collected books. I excelled at the subjects she taught, speech and drama. I was obsessed with Linda Carter as *Wonder Woman*. She saw it as part of my healthy heterosexual desire.

Despite her early observation of fairies in my soul, my mother's reaction to my coming out revealed limits to her

I didn't like. As the daughter of a man who served as the mayor and the newspaper publisher in their small Wisconsin town, she came at the world from a place of privilege, through the narrow prism of what others thought. She was the product of an era in which coming out was better wished away or shamed into silence.

It didn't cross her radar when the American Psychiatric Association eliminated "homosexuality" from its list of psychiatric illnesses in 1973. Being gay was a weakness. If I was going to be actor, she would have preferred me to be Paul Newman over Paul Lynde, or a writer, Mailer over Capote. She only wanted what every American mother wanted: a masculine son who could throw a football and live a normal, boring life.

"For Chrissakes, Mom. Your favorite musical is *A Chorus Line*. How could you be so tough on me?"

"Tough on you?!" She took a breath. Her voice dropped into stage whisper. "Please don't tell anyone else."

"You can't tell me who I can or cannot tell. What makes you think you're the first person I would tell, anyway? Suppose everyone knew? Huh? This isn't about you."

I'd already shared the truth about myself with a few people from high school and a handful of friends at NYU. My two brothers knew, my stepsiblings had their suspicions, everyone else was on their own. My mother's instant approval would have been aces—but despite her liberal leanings, I knew it was going to be a challenge.

First of all, her husband, my father's dim replacement, was a bigot. His favorite adjective was "fucking" and even though we lived in lily-white suburbia, he managed to toss off the n-word quite a bit. Around our house "faggot" was as common and interchangeable as "stupid." I'd been briefed on such language at the movies every Sunday with my dad. Although their usage, especially "around the kids," gave my mother a case of stage sighs, the words usually went unchallenged. My mother, when angry, used tame, old school exclamations: "Eat my shorts!" "Chrimanutleys!" "Heck's Beck's!" When truly angry, she would let loose a few choice words, hovering over them for a beat to emphasize she was using language beneath her. She wanted to say, "Well, fuck."

"I wish I'd had the chance to tell Dad," I said.

"What am I going to do about—"

"What you tell your husband is up to you."

"Well, Heck's Becks. This sure is a surprising turn of events."

"Is it, Mom? What exactly are you surprised about?"

"I…I just need some time to digest all of this."

"Do you remember what divorce was like, Mom?"

"Why would you ask—?"

"Because I'm about to divorce the lot of you."

I returned to New York, broke up with Ken, and replaced my studies with nightlife. The original Studio 54 was long gone, but a glut of hangar-sized spaces—The Palladium, The Tunnel, The Roxy, Underground, Limelight, Mars, filled with house music, designer drugs, and club kids—carried on the tradition despite the growing epidemic.

I found a $750-a-month five floor walk-up on East Houston between A and B with my friend, Raven-O, a Hawaiian-born drag superstar with ass-long tresses, almond eyes, and the legs of a female dancer.

I met Raven at the boy bar, a deliberately lowercase asylum of joy located on rough and raggedy St. Mark's Place. Part drag club, part twink bar, the two-story building—not counting the illegal basement dance floor—was lorded over by a heterosexual hairdresser rumored to be the inspiration for Warren Beatty's character in *Shampoo*.

On Thursday, Friday, and Saturday nights, boy bar showcased fierce performers who worked the fags into a froth: Glamamore, Sister Codie Ravioli, Perfidia, Flotilla DeBarge, Mona Foot, Candis Cayne.

Raven-O's regimented dance routines, like his step-for-step recreation of Janet Jackson's *Rhythm Nation 1814* choreography, wowed b-boys and sweater gays alike. His realness was unspookable and his ballsy offstage antics were legendary. Through Raven, I gained backstage access to watch the queens as they beat their faces and assembled their sequins, to laugh at their banter and their bitching.

H.R.H. Princess Diandra never failed with her spot-on impersonations of Whitney Houston, Patti LaBelle, and Diana Ross. Between songs, she liked to grab the microphone and unleash her tongue on the crowd, sparing no one.

Connie Girl brought madcap glamor to the boy bar. She could dance on point as easily as she could create a vaudevillian character or cartwheel her 6-foot frame, in 6-inch heels, across a stage the size of a twin bed. Later, she repurposed her flawless walk on Thierry Mugler's Paris runway.

Miss Guy, the Iggy Pop of drag, brought obscure rock'n'roll chicks to the fore. He eventually parlayed his fuck-you androgyny into an impressive, independent rock career.

The fairy godmother who transcended them all was International Chrysis. An ageless beauty, she appeared in *The Queen,* a groundbreaking documentary from 1968, as well as Sidney Lumet's *Q&A* in 1990. She was a muse to Dali in the 1970s, a buxom "intersexual" who delighted in showing off her ample jugs while bragging about her ten-inch dick.

"Ain't ever gonna' take away my moneymaker!" she'd laugh.

On Sunday nights, a few blocks east and a few blocks south at 101 Avenue A, Hapi Phace presided over the madness at "Whispers" at The Pyramid. Dressed in suburban housewife finest, with no attempt to disguise his true gender, Hapi Phace bantered with the audience between acts, tossing out the most godawful jokes. (Hapi: "Where are you from?" Audience member: "Queens." Hapi: "Queens?! I'm from normal parents.")

The Pyramid's atmosphere tended to be more

cerebral and more punk than boy bar, stressing performance over female illusion. Artists like Wendy Wild, John Sex, Ffloyd, Tabboo!, Sister Dimension, Billy Beyond, Olympia, Linda Simpson, and RuPaul rounded out the pantheon of Lower East Side drag royalty.

To label what was going on in those clubs as "drag" misses the point, of course. More than men prancing about as women for laughs, the East Village queens were performers of intense artistic expression, and like the queens of Stonewall, crucial political protestors willing to tell the truth through wicked satire and pop music hooks. They loaded their feminine illusion with feminist allusions. They were glittering satellites gloriously transiting a galaxy of their own making. With so much darkness around, we needed them desperately.

A few of the boy bar "beauties" crossed over to the Pyramid Club, but very few Pyramid queens performed on the boy bar stage. It was up to Lady Bunny—a hybrid of Joanne Worley and Dusty Springfield, known for her spirited staging of Salsoul anthems, scatalogical humor, and keen political diatribes—to gather all the queens, regardless of their nightlife affiliation or respective talents, into the bandshell at Thompkins Square Park for her annual end-of-summer dragfest, Wigstock.

One performer in particular, who went by the name of Chiclet, inspired me like no other. Before long, she became a sister to me. For Chiclet, looking real and lipsynching the words of hallowed divas were "clown shows." Chiclet sought shock over glamour. Fucking with gender was for amateurs; Chiclet wanted to fuck with the audience.

I don't recall the first time I saw Chiclet, but I'll never forget the performance that made me want to be her friend. It was another night at boy bar with Chiclet on the bill. As usual, no one had a clue what she would do. Even if the mc, Matthew Kasten, had announced, "Tonight, Chiclet will lipsynch Nina Hagen's *Naturträne*," we still wouldn't have had any idea what to expect.

The lights dimmed slowly as the eerily comforting opening chords of a strumming guitar quieted the buzzing crowd. A tight spotlight pinpointed Chiclet's powdered white nose, then expanded slowly to reveal enormous bug-eye sunglasses, glittering orange lips, and a black-and-blue fright wig. Nina's guttural German seemed to fly from Chiclet's mouth as if thrown up by one of Satan's angels.

Above the groaning guitar and steady drums, Chiclet's spotlight widened. She wore a cable-knit sweater striped in faded earth tones and a crumpled black skirt made from yards of pleather. Her right arm levitated slowly into a flat salute. On her wrist, a toy bug, covered in blue and black crystals, flapped its shining wings. The stage was disarmingly bare.

At the climax of the number ("Ooooooh, oooooh, oooooh, oooooh, oooooh, ooooooh, ECH! ECH!! AHA-HA! ECH!!!") Chiclet's body began to stretch upward, slowly, imperceptibly at first, then higher and higher until the top of her wig pressed against the crude lights jutting from the ceiling.

"Aaaaaah oooh aaaaahhhh . . ." Nina's voice wailed. Chiclet's skirt fluttered like a parachute. She spun like a dervish. Hoots and hollers from the audience drowned out Nina's voice as she ended her song with the cluck of a chicken. Blackout. Whistles and screams.

Backstage, away from the mystified audience, Raven emerged, sweaty and winded, from under Chiclet's voluminous skirt. No one in the audience ever knew—or was too wasted to care—how Chiclet grew, or that Raven provided the mechanics. Chiclet called the number "Bach Bock." Promoters booked the act at every nightclub in town until Raven would no longer provide the mechanics.

Chiclet was reared upstate by parents who supported their son unconditionally—including her eventual decision to transition to female. Chiclet served her time as a drag queen before changing her name to Adriana and embarking on life as a woman 24/7.

At the time, I worked as the monitor for a group of phone sex lines in a high-rise overlooking the United Nations. My boss was a queer Quaker from Boston, a pioneer in the burgeoning industry of pay-to-listen pornography.

In my official duties as monitor, I was on the lookout to disconnect crank callers with the push of a button. I was also expected to connect couples who struck it off—they would press a button on their phone that would signal me to switch them to a "private room" to continue their conversation. Eight hours a day for five days a week,

I slipped surreptitiously from group conversation to group conversation: from 550-TOOL for "leathermen," to 550-STUD for the "straight-acting, straight-looking, VGL, UB2s" that once littered personals sections.

The most popular line was 550-TVTS, advertised as the line for "chicks with dicks and their admirers." Chiclet/Adriana and Lady Bunny were quickly hired for their canny abilities to keep the male-identified callers hanging on, at 15 cents a minute each, for entire 8-hour shifts.

It was around this time that I made my first visit to St. Vincent's Hospital. On a humid Friday evening, Raven and I, propelled through a marathon night of house parties on a mix of vodka shots and sake, ended up at the latest "Outlaw Party," a flash-mob event orchestrated by a club kid who later killed and dismembered a man in an episode that changed New York's nightlife forever.

The party took place on the abandoned elevated train tracks that terminated at Gansevoort Street. There were massive cracks in the concrete slabs used to replace rusted-out steel beams, ankle-snapping holes hidden by sea grasses and the dried-out carcasses of climbing wildflowers. Some people brought beat boxes and danced, but most stood around and chatted. Basically, it was a bore on a packed, abandoned bridge until sirens pierced the muffled din and police cruisers began to arrive. Queens acted up like Shelley Winters in *The Poseidon Adventure*. Despite bullhorn warnings requesting a calm exit down the rickety steps, there was panic. Some shimmied down the metal columns or dashed off further down the untamed train tracks. People dropped to their hands and knees and crawled, their silhouettes disappearing into the shaking weeds. Drunken screams of pain and peals of laughter filled the night.

Raven and I were at the ledge overlooking the slick cobblestones of Gansevoort Street. To the left of us, a long line formed for the stairs. To the right, a railing separated us from the street. Without hesitation, Raven scaled the railing and glided to the sidewalk like Spiderman.

He landed on his feet before falling backwards. He stood up quickly. "Come on!" he shouted, dusting off the butt of his bondage pants. He realigned the zippers and buckles. "Come on, pussy! It's nothing!!"

I lacked the grace of my roommate and doubted I could survive a two-story fall without breaking both of my legs, but the vodka and the sake in my system persuaded me. I eased my way over the railing and hesitated on the other side. Raven paced in small circles below.

"Pussy! Hurry up!"

I closed my eyes and jumped. The heels of my Doc Martens struck the concrete with a smack before sliding out from under me. I landed on my tailbone. I tried to stand, but the pain was so intense I fell back onto the sidewalk. I wasn't sure what hurt the most: my busted ankle, my bruised tailbone, or my humiliated ego. A crowd of freaks began to crowd around me as if I was part of the evening's entertainment.

"Come on, move along, people!" cops shouted. I wasn't able to move at all.

A stray voice asked if I needed an ambulance. Embarrassed, I shrugged the suggestion off. Plus, the night was still young. I didn't want to waste it in the emergency room at St. Vincent's. That's when I realized it was my friend Kevin's voice. Kevin was a fellow boy bar habitué who worked evenings as a caregiver for a rich guy with Lou Gehrig's disease. He'd arrived at the Outlaw Party too late. He hadn't seen my fall, just the aftermath. I was like a wounded pigeon in all the chaos.

With the assistance of Raven and Kevin, I hobbled down the uneven Belgian blocks of Gansevoort toward the only light on the block, a pink neon glow radiating from a large steamy window. As we got closer, I realized we were headed to Restaurant Florent.

Two payphones occupied by wildly gesticulating drag queens and a cigarette machine the size of a Harley stood along the wall in the cramped entryway. Beyond the wide strips of heavy plastic that hung in the doorframe was a long dining room paneled with the quilted stainless steel of American proletariat diners.

Obscure divas wailed from the speakers above the cacophonous chatter of customers, the clanging of overstuffed busboy tubs and screams of "Pick up!" from the half-door that led to the kitchen.

According to the warning posted behind the bar, between the cash register and a notice to pregnant

57

women that drinking causes birth defects, the restaurant was beyond its occupancy limit of 199 persons. Every seat of the restaurant's 20 tables and two long counters was filled with someone without plans of leaving. Up front, a small, colorful mob waited in vain to replace them. Especially after midnight, the restaurant seemed like a set out of *Bladerunner*, caught in a permafrost of '80s cool. With the lure of a free pack of Kool Lights, we persuaded one of the queens to abandon her post at one of the pay phones to call Kevin's client's fancy car service.

That's how I arrived at the emergency room of St. Vincent's in the back seat of a shiny black 1989 Chrysler New Yorker. It wasn't very dramatic: no gunshot victims, no subway stabbings, no other fools from the Outlaw Party. They were on to the next event.

A bone-thin man with sunken eyes and a John Waters moustache held hands with another man, not as thin, eyes far more alert and wet with tears. An i.v. pole stood between them, holding a ringer bag of sugar water that dripped out the time. They were clearly waiting for a room to open up on the 7th floor.

I filled out some paperwork. No one blinked when I said I had no insurance. They examined me, wrapped my swollen, blue ankle in a bandage, and handed me a pair of crutches. No one ever asked for money, and I never received a bill.

About six months later, Raven got me a job on the overnight shift at Restaurant Florent, which I parlayed into a dinner shift bussing tables, paying my dues until a highly-coveted waiting shift materialized. On New Year's Eve of 1990, I scored the lucrative low-work gig of checking coats at the restaurant, which meant sitting in a tiny utility closet in the back between unisex toilets with doors marked "WC," charging $2 an item with a large tip jar visible.

Earlier that day I woke up raspy, my mouth and chest raw and dry. I blamed it on the old steam heat radiator in my apartment. When I left to work the coat check that evening, my throat was burning. I had a chamomile tea with honey and lemon and a few shots of whiskey as the waiters and busboys, all in 1940's musical drag, prepared for the evening ahead of us. But it only grew worse. Co-workers joked that I had gonorrhea of the throat. It hurt so much I thought that I might.

Despite the pain, I suffered through ten hours of demanding drunks packed into a space the size of a railcar celebrating 1990. After I assembled my tips, I walked over to the St. Vincent's emergency room. It was predictably crowded. The triage nurse asked me to take a seat in the packed waiting room. Kathie Lee and Regis chatted on the large tv in the corner, both still drunk from New Year's Eve festivities.

Around 10 am I was told an intern would see me. After a brief once-over, she wondered if might have streptococcal pharyngitis. She swabbed the back of my throat for a culture and sent it to the lab. She wrote me a prescription for amoxicillin, told me to drink fluids and suck on lozenges. As she predicted, it cleared up within a few days. Just like the last time, I had no insurance, yet I never received a bill. I also never went in for a proper follow-up.

About nine months later, on a clear September evening, my co-workers and I were setting up for the dinner shift and attending to the few stragglers who had wandered in for midday snacks. The chef on-duty, MaryLou, and I discussed children, specifically the child she and her partner, Lisa, hoped to have by the following September.

The two had just moved in together. "That seems like a big step," I said.

"Well, we figure since we're not permitted to get married, at the least we can share in the life of a child together."

I stacked folded napkins on the counter. MaryLou wrote out her specials for the night. She smacked a set of index cards against the counter and pushed her pen into her thick hair. I grabbed for the forks.

"How 'bout you? What do you think of having a kid?"

"Me?" I laughed. "I can't even manage a dog."

She clicked her tongue. "We'd make beautiful kids, though. My German and Puerto Rican genes. Your blue eyes."

I'd never thought about it before. Watching my siblings and a number of friends struggle with kids in a fucked-up world, I was relieved to be free of that burden.

But to have a kid with a lesbian couple? That would be ideal. Outside of jerking off into a cup and scheduling weekly play dates, no real responsibilities involved. The moms do all the real work, and I get to help guide a little version of myself through the world. That's the kind of kid I could have.

"Of course," said Lisa, when the three of us met a few days later to hammer out the details, "you'll need to get tested."

I'd taken an HIV test the year before at the New York City Department of Health Clinic on 9th Avenue and 22nd Street. By law, to be tested you had to give a name to your caseworker. However, there was no law requiring caseworkers to ask for identification—and they never did. Following the trend of the time, I gave my name as Nancy Reagan. Two weeks later, the results came back negative.

"You could get tested over in Jersey," suggested MaryLou. "There you can be truly anonymous. They give you a number. No need to lie and say you're Bonzo's wife."

"Bonzo was the monkey," said Lisa.

"Whatever. We'll drive you to Jersey City. In and out. We'll grab lunch, make a day of it. Two weeks later, we'll go back and get the results."

To deal with the two-week waiting period, I went out every night of the week after the dinner shift. When I got too drunk, I'd smoke cigarettes and snort coke until the morning grew too harsh, and sleep was the only way out.

When I emerged with my Jersey City results that day, I told MaryLou and Lisa, "I guess I'm just not meant to be a father." My positive status was no surprise. The real shock came a month later when I visited the Community Health Project in the Gay and Lesbian Center and discovered that my immune system was on already on the wane. A random doctor, assigned to give me the results of my disappointing blood work, shook his head in frustration when he told me I had two CD4+ T-lymphocytes, or "T-cells." I named them "Abbott and Costello." According to the Centers for Disease Control, the pair made me a prime candidate for AIDS.

"Don't kid yourself," warned the doctor. "This is going to kill you. It's going to make you very sick and you will die a horrible death if you do nothing. AZT is all we have right now. It slows the progression of the virus. Do you want to go blind? Do you want to be covered in Kaposi sarcoma? It's your only chance of survival."

I refused. AZT was poison, and HIV was a correlation, not causation. There was more than just a virus responsible for the 26 diseases that constituted my newest obstacles. Drinking, smoking, drugs, stress, diet, exercise, sleep, self-esteem: these things mattered to the immune system too. The counselor in New Jersey said that he noticed a higher rate of illness and death in HIV-positive people who continued to use cocaine. When I told him I'd stop right away, he said, "That's a start."

I read about guys who had turned to alternative therapies and mental health counseling to increase their chances of survival. I told the red-faced doctor I wanted to follow their lead.

"Those are just anecdotes," he sneered.

"I'd rather be an anecdote than a statistic."

FRANNY & JOEY
(1967)

"This war in Vietnam is, I believe, a war for civilization."
—Cardinal Francis Spellman, 1966

Drifting in and out of morphine visions and desperate to breathe on his own, Cardinal Francis Spellman had the stark realization he might not be around for Christmas. The doctors at St. Vincent's, and more than a few specialists brought over from other hospitals, had all but given up on the old man, but the Sisters of Charity remained hopeful and catered to His Eminence's every whim.

One morning, the door to his room opened and a wall of white roses speckled with red appeared. Behind the outlandish arrangement was his dear friend, Roy Cohn, fresh off the train from D.C.

"You shouldn't have," chuckled the cardinal through

his oxygen mask. "That's enough for a few men's funerals."

Roy laughed. His Eminence enjoyed Roy's company. With Roy, he could speak with his zucchetto off.

The two reminisced about their Italian summer so many years ago, how they'd snuck out of the Vatican to head to Florence where they watched brutal, muscled Italians play harpastum.

"Oh, Franny," Roy laughed. "What I wouldn't give for one of those young calcianti these days. With a big fat cannoli!"

Franny sighed. "It seems my days of frolic are over."

Roy had never seen fear in his friend's face. He touched his shoulder and searched for something to say.

"Do not go gentle into that good night," he finally said, with as much sentiment as he could muster.

Franny winced. "Please don't. Dylan Thomas died here, you know."

"Is that right?"

"Thank you for the roses, Roy."

"You like'em? I'm glad. They cost me enough. Are they fragrant?"

Franny pointed at his oxygen mask. He shook his head. Impossible.

Roy stood and buried his nose in one of the opened buds. He grimaced. "The beautiful ones never stink good."

Franny thought of Joey. The way Joey smelled. No matter how much rose water the boy dowsed upon himself he could never conceal his juvenile musk. When he emerged from the limousine in the evenings from his whirlwind performances in *One Touch of Venus* at the Imperial, he smelled of dance belts and greasepaint.

They met backstage on opening night. Agnes DeMille enjoyed telling people how she introduced the cardinal to the chorus boy. His Eminence told Joey that he found the book a little wanting. The songs were good enough and the dancing was excellent and although he preferred Dietrich in the film—and would have loved to see her do it onstage—he tolerated Mary Martin's performance just fine. What struck His Eminence most were the show's ballets, especially Joey's lithe build and divine range of motion.

One Touch of Venus closed on February 10, 1945 after 567 performances. Since that time, His Eminence kept Joey in an apartment on Park Avenue within walking distance of St. Patrick's Cathedral. The odd couple spent most evenings together for nearly seven years. Outside of a few friends from the monastery, it was the longest sustained relationship His Eminence had experienced. He loved Joey as far as the Lord—and discretion—would allow. He knew Joey could never love His Eminence. Not because he was a man of the cloth more than twice his age. Joey could never love Franny because Joey couldn't love himself.

"Franny! Franny! Are you still with me?"

"For the time being, Roy, I am still with you."

"We're still 'together,' we'll always be 'together,'" Joey

said as he threw clothes into his suitcase. Booked on a cross-country tour, Joey was having a hard time packing for the weather of both Miami and Minneapolis. He didn't need the old man's histrionics.

"But you're *leaving*, Joey." The cardinal had the ear of the Pope. He had a direct line to world leaders, especially President Truman. He had the unfettered support of the wealthiest families in New York. Yet there was self-pity in his voice. Joey found the sudden pathos unbecoming.

"I have to work, Franny. I can't get a show on Broadway. I've been auditioning my ass off for years now and all I've gotten is old."

"You're only 29."

"I'm almost 32."

"You'd be better than that bald Russian at the St. James."

"Are you even listening to me? I'm no Yul Brynner. I'm just a chorus boy—"

"Joseph! You're much more than that!"

"I'm a performer, Francis. For audiences—not just for you."

In his wildest nightmares, Franny never thought Joey would leave, much less vanish overnight. A thin envelope arrived from Los Angeles on June 29, 1952. It was over. Every day since then, His Eminence said a prayer for Joey. Every night, Joey haunted his dreams.

In 1964, when the cardinal turned 75, he asked the pope if he might retire. His request was declined. His Eminence had never felt so desperate.

After deep reflection, he turned his attention full-barrel to the anti-communist skirmish in Indochina. He harangued President Johnson and the muddled Congress. Tragic as it was, the Gulf of Tonkin incident answered the cardinal's prayers. Some wags took to calling Viet Nam, "Spelly's War," which His Eminence found repugnant. He despised the liberals—recently assassinated presidents included—who would capitulate to the Communist threat rather than take up arms and squelch it. If he needed to be a martyr for the world's freedom, so be it. They make saints out of men for less.

"You know the story of Lazarus, don't you, Roy?"

Roy was startled. He thought his old friend had fallen asleep and was trying to make a quiet exit from the room. "If it's in the Old Testament, I'm sure it's passed through my brain pan."

"I was thinking how difficult it must have been. For Lazarus. To accept your fate. To slip off the mortal coil. To find peace from the quotidian. To trade the tragedy of existence for eternal joy. And just as you are laid away to rest for eternity, Jesus shows up, rolls away your tombstone, and commands you to walk."

"Kind of a rude awakening, sounds to me," answered Roy, still standing near the doorway. Franny heaved in seizures and unleashed a barrage of tears. Roy closed the door and returned to the bedside.

"I still think about Joey," His Eminence confessed. He sniffled and wiped his face. "I must seem a fool."

Roy leaned over and kissed the cardinal's forehead.

"Don't you worry. I'll make sure no one tries to open up your goddamned tomb."

Franny's lungs struggled to let out a cackle. Roy laughed with his old friend one last time.

BECAUSE IT IS BITTER

"In the desert
I saw a creature, naked, bestial,
Who, squatting upon the ground,
Held his heart in his hands,
And ate of it.
I said, 'Is it good, friend?'
'It is bitter—bitter,' he answered;
'But I like it
'Because it is bitter,
'And because it is my heart.'"

—Stephen Crane,
In the Desert

Nearly every day, from my sublet on the far edge of Prospect Park, I biked eight miles to and from a sleek sustainable loft on lower Broadway that housed Marianne Williamson's Manhattan Center for Living. With a group of "dis-eased" contrarians, I dined on macrobiotic lunches and attended Qi-Gong classes, free to explore alternatives to the extremely limited response provided by

Western medicine. At the Manhattan Center for Living, we were encouraged to cure ourselves without any assistance from Big Pharma.

One day, I found myself swept up into a standing-room-only Q&A with "Ronnie," a handsome, HIV-positive guy who told us about his regimen of bitter melon tea enemas and his subsequent 600-percent increase in t-4 helper cells. As a bonus, his unorthodox procedure had boosted mood, energy, and sex drive. All within a single year.

As a buzz swept through the room, an older, shorter man with the stillness of a yogi stood up and introduced himself as Dr. Xeng. He spoke about bitter melon's medicinal properties and its restorative effects on ailing immune systems. He recounted a few stories similar to Ronnie's and asked if there might be any potential subjects in the room willing to undergo daily bitter tea melon enemas. Hands went up like surrender flags.

Sure, we were skeptical, but many of us were desperate enough to swallow balloons of Drain-O if it meant getting better. I was one of thirty guinea pigs to sign up for Dr. Xeng's bitter melon tea enema study.

We were asked to keep journals to document our experiences, including ounces absorbed, amount of time retained, physical reactions, moods, feelings, dietary issues, gas bubbles, the occurrence of leaks. We also recorded our blood work numbers. I titled my journal, *Because It Is Bitter and Because It Is My Melon.*

The whole wretched enterprise lasted about three

months. My last entry from *Because It Is Bitter*, the week after Labor Day 1994, reads, "Ran 6 miles Prospect Park; after lukewarm bath, assumed plough position and retained 16 oz. for half hour period."

"Phone rang around 15-minute mark," it continues. "Preoccupied as I was, I screened. It was Ken. He said he was out on the island with Bobby and wanted to ask me a question."

I lay in the middle of the living room in the shape of a folded jackknife, ankles at my ears, bare ass in the air, bitter melon tea solution doing its immuno-enhancing magic through the lining of my small intestine—or so I wanted to believe.

I had no desire to speak with Ken; he had no desire to speak with me. I only called back to find out what Bobby wanted. I loved the man. I'd heard that his health had deteriorated.

"I could live the rest of my life without Ken, but Bobby is still my fairy godfather," I wrote. Besides that life-changing 19th birthday at their house in the Pines, I saw Bobby and Stewart for monthly dinners at Empire Szechuan when Ken and I were together, and he always sent me postcards from glamorous locales: Mykonos, Thailand, Barcelona.

On the fourth ring, a nasal dial tone of a voice answered. It was Timmy, Bobby's best friend and Ken's nemesis.

"Hi doll. How's tricks," he said flatly. Before I had a chance to answer, he continued, "I'll get Ken-Doll. Hold tight." He laid the receiver down. The house was silent. Then I heard Ken sigh.

"Hello?"

"You sound so strained. Just to talk to me?"

"Look," he replied in a stern whisper. He despised banter and was not up for mine. "This is Bobby's idea. I'm against it. I'm arranging this under protest."

"Arranging what?"

"Bobby's not well. You know that. He's not getting better and he refuses to listen to his doctors or me or common sense. He'd like to spend the winter in Hawaii. On Maui. Uh ... he wanted me to ask you to join him. He, uh, figures you could write, or something. He just needs someone around, help him get to doctor's appointments, uh, whatever. He'd like to meet with you when he gets back to the city. Probably next week or so. That is, if you have nothing else going on."

Bobby and Ken knew I made my living by dying. The city's Division of AIDS Services covered my rent. The Manhattan Center for Living fed me macrobiotic lunches. The Gay Men's Health Crisis provided free tickets to Broadway shows and concerts now and then to keep me from going out of my skull. I collected disability checks from Social Security and used food stamps at the Park Slope Food Co-op.

A few days a week, I volunteered at DAAIR (Direct AIDS Alternative Information Resources), a buyers club for contrarians, where we doled out black walnut tinctures for gastrointestinal parasites, milk thistle

73

capsules for liver conditions, black licorice capsules to bolster the immune system ... I answered questions, completed orders, broke down cardboard boxes, stocked the shelves that lined every available inch of our cramped headquarters, which doubled as the founder's one-bedroom apartment.

Bobby and Ken knew I had nothing to lose and quite a bit to gain from leaving the city for the winter. I was as good a caretaker as any. I didn't have a heroin addiction or a drinking problem. I was a pretty good cook. Relatively quiet. Unemployed. Most importantly, Bobby trusted me.

When we met to plan our upcoming winter, it was clear he was experiencing more than the after-effects of a stroke. Specialists, neurologists, and multiple MRIs knew his brain was shrinking. They had no idea why. It started in the brain stem and moved into the cerebellum. "Like expanding air bubbles" is how he described it. "Looks like Swiss cheese."

I could not be certain that his crumbling condition was solely the result of the ever-widening fissures in his brain or if he was taking too many triplicates.

The left side of his face drooped as if he'd suffered a stroke. Bumps of molluscum contagiosa, also known as water warts, speckled his 5 o'clock shadow. Froth ringed his lips. He was slow to form words and unable to walk more than a few steps at a time. Despite these conditions, his skin was bronze. Bobby always kept the tan that tied him to his glorious youth, regardless of his illness. His appetite never waned, and his upper body remained thick and firm, which only encouraged the common misconception that his slurred words were caused by too much drink.

He stood with some effort to hug me when I entered the apartment. He was smaller than he was when we first met at his house on Neptune Walk in August of 1986. Bobby wanted to make sure I understood his wishes, so sis best friend Timmy joined us, hovering about the living room like a chaperone and enunciating words Bobby couldn't quite get out of his mouth.

First order of business: Bobby didn't want to end up like all those guys—masked, tubed, horizontal—on the 7th floor of St. Vincent's.

He also didn't want to be saved by qi gong, macrobiotics, or bitter melon enemas.

Most importantly, in the clearest sentence he spoke that afternoon, "I wanna' go when it's time to go."

My responsibility, Timmy explained, was to make sure Bobby had whatever he needed to be comfortable until that time came. And when it did, I promised them both I'd get Bobby back to his bed in New York. I'd make the proper phone calls. I'd make sure he left this world on his own terms. And I would tell no one, including Ken, who did not condone Bobby's hoarding of Seconals as end-of-life planning.

Initially, Bobby wanted to live out his final days on Maui, but a six-month quarantine for Joe, his beloved Brussels Griffin, put an end to that fantasy. After some coercion, Bobby reluctantly agreed to Florida as a compromise. Timmy and Bobby's primary physician, Dr. Braun, agreed that Key West would be "a closer alternative."

"Gay elephant graveyard," mumbled Bobby, when the location was decided.

From Bobby's lawyer's point of view, being in the same time zone would allow them to finish Bobby's last will and testament, a fickle project that Bobby dragged out on purpose. Even though the man had no real assets, he wanted to make sure he chose his beneficiaries well. It was important to Bobby that his remaining possessions— furniture, books, artwork—end up in the right hands. Most of the people Bobby met over the course of his half-century of life were dead, dying, or as in the case of his family, on his shit list. Bobby was giving them the chance to make good.

For four months, Bobby, Joe, and I lived a situation tragedy about two queers and a dog named Joe making their way in a three-bedroom ranch house in Old Town with a saltwater pool and a courtyard of hibiscus, antherium, bouganvillea, and palm trees to give Joe a place to relieve himself and Bobby the feeling of being in Hawaii. Our first item on the agenda was amassing a battery of Key West doctors. Just like their peers in New York, the island doctors were overworked and overbooked. Bobby's only concern was that they be willing to overprescribe.

The second item on our agenda was getting Bobby a

"Jazzy." He was tired of the walker Dr. Braun had suggested, and he was dying anyway; why not ride around town like all the ancient diabetics from the docked cruise ships?

Bobby's hearing was one of the next things to go. By sunset, CNN would rise to the highest possible volume. Whatever I prepared for dinner was no match against the white, male hotheads of *Crossfire* screaming at each other on maximum volume. Even poor Joe sought sanctuary from the meshugas and hid out in the garden.

In the beginning I tried to engage in a discussion against AZT or dismiss the effectiveness of Bactrim prophylaxis. Bobby would nod and smile and shrug. "You may be rie." What he wanted to say, if only he could pronounce his words properly, was "Don't you get it? You frightened young man. AIDS didn't start with Rock Hudson. It was around long before either of us heard about it."

Bobby knew dozens of people personally who had died since it was called "gay cancer." Some claimed their Kaposi sarcoma lesions were the result of popper use and sun damage, not sex, as they sauntered off to the St. Mark Baths. Then he watched them die. My denials sounded especially hollow.

Stewart ended his days hooked up to an oxygen tank, still claiming, between hits of aerosolized Pentamadine, that the pneumocystis carnii pneumonia destroying his lungs was caused by pot tainted by Paraquat.

Even Keith, smart, young, beautiful Keith, Bobby's

surprise second chance at love after Stewart's death, claimed his rapid weight loss and jaundiced cast were the results of hepatitis and a strict juicing regimen. He died from liver failure on the 7th floor of St. Vincent's within days of his admittance.

Bobby heard every entitled excuse from every queen he knew. He shook his head at every crackpot theory and every method of denial. He knew it was human to deny, to deflect, to shift focus. People will grab hold of anything when they're scared. The sick convince themselves they're different, what they have is curable, benign. What they have won't wipe them off the map as wickedly as it had their friends. The healthy convince themselves they won't be affected.

Despite Bobby's obvious discomfort, we had a pleasant couple of months. We both made an effort to make Christmas joyous. By the end of January, Bobby was unable to utter anything resembling human speech. His organs were no longer under his control. Walking was impossible, and his hands shook too badly to hold the remote control. Forget reading.

At breakfast one balmy morning in early February, without saying a word, he made it clear: no need to pack up the house, get us a flight to New York now.

Like most gay men of his generation, Bobby would have preferred to die young and leave a beautiful corpse, but the chance for that cliché was long over. He was sick of being sick. Sick of being ugly and disabled. He refused to wait out the end of his life at St. Vincent's or at some hospice outside of his beloved Manhattan. Bobby opted for quality, not quantity, and even in death, he insisted on control.

Back in New York, Bobby instructed me to gather his lawyer, his best friend, Timmy, and a couple of witnesses. While they completed Bobby's will, I took a nap in the guest bedroom beneath the stuffed blue sailfish that hung on the wall.

When I woke up, Timmy was rummaging through the kitchen cabinets. He was looking for Bobby's Mason jar of Seconals. The doctor had already shown up and given Bobby two shots, an antiemetic and an opioid.

"So, I guess this is it," Timmy said.

I opened the cabinet above the refrigerator and handed Timmy the Mason jar half-full of pink pills. I took a pint of Cherry Garcia out of the freezer and grabbed a spoon from the drawer.

Bobby laughed when we entered the bedroom. He motioned for Timmy to leave. Timmy stood still for a moment. He jerked forward awkwardly and leaned over his friend. Bobby shook his head, no. Timmy kissed him on the lips.

"Save a spot for me," he whispered, then darted from the room.

Joe watched the proceedings with knowing eyes before burrowing his snout into Bobby's chest. Bobby stroked his head. He motioned to me that the room was hot. I opened the sliding glass doors at the foot of his bed.

In the winter haze, the Grace Church steeple looked like a glowing peak of melted wax. The air was surprisingly mild and still, dense with anticipation. We had escaped to Key West because the previous winter had been brutal, yet it felt like the kind of winter that make people feel thankful for global warming.

I sat on the edge of Bobby's bed and fed him spoons full of ice cream. Joe licked his lips. Bobby's head sank into his pillows. He lolled his tongue about in ecstasy. He chewed each chocolate chunk, every frozen cherry, with meaning, coating his taste buds thoroughly before raising his head for more.

After nearly half of the pint, Bobby waved the spoon away. I placed the sweating container beside a large bottle of Evian on the nightstand and opened the Mason jar. Bobby reached for it with a shaking hand. He tried to grab a handful, but the pink elliptical pills fell from his cupped left palm and bounced off his distended rib cage into the sheets. I dug around to retrieve them before Joe could.

Bobby pinched a couple between his fingers. On their way to his open mouth, his hand convulsed and they fell again. He moaned in frustration. He gyrated his head until his pillows began to shift. "Heh me," he said.

I placed two more Seconals on his dry white tongue. He signaled for water. I hadn't opened the bottle yet or poured any into the glass. As I did, he made choking sounds. I must have looked at him in a panic. He managed a smile and laughed. I brought the glass to his lips and waited for him to swallow.

"Tah to me," he said.

I couldn't think of anything to say. "This reminds me of communion."

"Me, too," he replied. "A-meh!"

"Yeah. Amen."

Bobby's parents had remained together for 47 years, and he and his brother were fairly close. He was almost embarrassed over his somewhat normal upbringing. He loved to hear me talk about my shitty childhood. Being tossed around like a football by older brothers, lipsynching The Go-Gos with my older sisters, having my face ripped open by a dog when I was four. He could no longer read, hated to be left with his own thoughts, and the endless O.J. trial coverage bored him. My tales of ostracism and abuse were his favorite entertainment that winter.

"Ushtanashin," he'd usually say when I finished a story, even though none of them were really "astonishing."

His crooked smile wept a stream of water. "Teh me abow beeng a preeesth."

He loved when I told the story of how I wanted to be a priest. Since I didn't fit in, I found solace in the rituals of being an altar boy. Layering the starched white cassock over the flowing red vestment alongside other boys in the sacristy. Listening to prayers for the next cue. The ceremonial footwork. Holding up the big book like a human podium. The call and response. The smell of incense on holy days and at funerals. Lighting the tall candles and snuffing out the wicks. White smoke snaking into mutant helices in the hushed air of St. Gilbert's.

Bobby shook his head. "Nah a ree sain."

"He is, too!" I laughed, falling for the same old line. "Gilbert of Sepringham, lord turned holy man. He was a real saint! He aided Thomas Becket against King Henry II. He was canonized by Pope Innocent III." I popped another pill onto his waiting tongue. "Or at least that's what they told me. I don't recall if his character made it into *The Lion in Winter*."

Bobby took a sip. I gave him another pill. "And rumor was, my fourth grade teacher, a very old nun named Sister Gilbertetta, was actually married to St. Gilbert. Why else would she take his name?"

After Bobby swallowed, he laughed and stuck out his tongue. Pill, sip, swallow.

I continued what had now become a monologue. "When we got Sister Virginine in the sixth grade, all the girls were sequestered to get the lowdown on their new monthly friends. Meanwhile, Father Harry took all the boys to a room near the sacristy and wrote the word 'SEMEN' in big letters across the chalkboard."

Tongue, pill, sip, swallow.

"He said, 'Boys, there comes a time in every man's life when he must choose his calling. The Church teaches us that there are only two roads a man may take: find a woman, marry, settle down, and raise a family, or do as I chose and join the priesthood to spread the

Holy Gospel.' "

Tongue, pill, sip, swallow.

" 'Semen,' he said, tapping the chalk against the word. "Semen, from the Latin, *serere*, to sow. Semen, in Latin, is seed. Man may choose to use his seed to give life to a woman's egg.' He then turned to the board again and wrote 'seminary' underneath 'semen.' "

Laugh. Tongue, pill, sip, swallow.

" 'And seminary,' Father told us, 'is a place where men of true faith gather to plant the word of the Lord. Both words come from the same Latin root. They are the only options that a man may choose. Become a father like your fathers, or become a father like me.' "

Tongue, pill, sip, swallow. Bobby's eyelids drooped. Seconds later, he forced himself to smile.

"And I knew, ain't no way I'm going to get married and have kids and get divorced and all that. So, I go home that night and announce to my mother that I wish to be a priest. She was ecstatic."

Laugh. Tongue, pill, sip, swallow, grimace. It was clear the swallowing was getting harder. He looked up at me and nodded. "Untih Herahdo."

"Until Geraldo Rivera reported from the dance floor of Studio 54 to a slack-jawed Hugh Downs on *20/20* and I saw fags dancing together with their shirts off. The third option."

Bobby laughed, a low sputter that shook his entire body; his lips glistened with spittle. "Ushtanashah," was the last thing I heard him say.

I must have fallen asleep shortly after. I woke to Joe whimpering. He remained perched on Bobby's chest; his left paw scratched at Bobby's chin. Timmy stood in the doorway.

I stood up and closed the sliding glass door. Timmy placed his hand on my shoulder as I walked to the other bedroom where I collapsed. At some point, the doctor returned to issue a death certificate, and Timmy called the crematorium. Bobby's body was gone by the time I woke up twelve hours later.

Of course, Bobby's family was more than shocked to hear the news. Primarily they were offended that we returned to the city without letting them know. Then his mother accused Timmy and I of conspiring to kill her son for money.

Bobby led everyone to believe that he owned the penthouse. The truth was, only after a team of lawyers fought to keep the rent-stabilized apartment in his name after his partner Stewart passed away in 1989 was he able to remain there. No one knew that his lifestyle was supported by overextended credit cards and cashed-in viatical settlements from the insurance policies he was wise enough to snatch up in the early days of the plague.

Bobby couldn't leave the lease to the penthouse on East 10th Street to me. Although he and Stewart set a precedent in the courts establishing same-sex partners equal to traditional spouses with regard to lease agreements, I was never Bobby's partner, and there was no way to prove I was. Instead, Bobby left me $9,999, the maximum amount he could bestow without jeopardizing the disability payments and Medicaid benefits I received. He wanted me to continue to live there—mostly to piss off the management company that had tried to evict him when Stewart died. Bobby wanted me to use the $9,999 to retain his lawyer and keep up the fight.

Ken, livid, never spoke to me again.

VILLA MISERIA
(1970)

"Any way you look at it, Diego Vinales was pushed. We are all being pushed."
—Gay Activists Alliance pamphlet,
March 8, 1970

Alfredo Diego Vinales did not like the father he had been named after. Around the age of ten, after his old man disappeared, the quiet, clever boy requested he be called by his middle name.

With his mother and two younger brothers, Diego endured a tough life in one of the villas miserias that ringed Bueno Aires. Inside him burned a desire to escape, fueled by the dog-eared pages of a battered book he carried with him at all times, *Una Guia de Nuevo York del Viajero.*

Actually, it was only half a book. He salvaged it one sultry evening as he and his brothers sifted through the landfill. It contained enough pictures and information to furnish Diego's imagination with skyscrapers, sidewalks, soda fountains, and enormous train stations full of people going places, wearing suits and hats, carrying handled boxes and bags of all shapes and sizes, in which Diego imagined they carried money.

While other boys played futbol with plastic bags bound with recycled string from the butcher, Diego preferred to fetch water for his mother, help out his five aunts in their ramshackle cucinas, or pore over images of the landmarks of Nueva York.

Aside from being gentle, Diego was known for his beauty. Everyone teased him about his mariposa eyelashes, cetrino eyes, and bee-stung lips. Diego avoided most people, choosing to keep his head down and ponder paths to freedom, to New York City, where such attributes might be considered an asset, not a hindrance.

On his 16th birthday, Diego stood 1.8-meters. He was taller than all but two men and one woman in his village. His head was a mop of lazy curls; his shoulders and back resembled a Roman statue. Women swooned as he carried buckets, shirtless, to and from the well down the main stone street.

Diego was never a student. He hadn't been in a classroom since he was twelve. Despite his daily chores, he wasn't what the Revolucion considered a worker. Diego was apolitical. He just wanted to get by—and eventually get out.

Diego didn't buy into the Church either, even though

he escorted his mother and her five sisters to services three times a week.

What Diego believed more than anything was the salvation that awaited him in New York. He'd heard about certain boys, "puta-timadors," who hung out around the Teatro Colon, waiting for wealthy men to pay for their company. Rumors swirled that a few of these hustlers managed to parlay their evenings into tickets out of Argentina. Some were said to be living in luxury in far-flung places like Tokyo and Montreal. After working up some courage, Diego headed for the opera house to try his luck.

It was a drizzly Saturday evening in August 1967, when Diego was approached by a handsome, older American businessman named Jim.

"Do you like the opera?" Jim asked, in his best Spanish.

Diego laughed softly. He lowered his head and shook it, no. He had never seen a man who looked as if he'd walked out of an alcohol advertisement speak Spanish, however haltingly. And what was that strange accent?

Diego knew that the man was interested in more than the opera. As the rain started to fall in earnest, he found himself caught up in a situation he had not thought through completely. Jim asked Diego if he'd like to join him for coffee. Diego had no idea what to do with such a proposition. He'd never "gone for coffee." Coffee was a needless luxury. The water that went into making a single cup of coffee could keep his family's needs satiated for a week. And he'd never sat in a cafe. He never had the money, the time—or the idea that he could.

Come, said Jim, leading Diego to a corner café. They sat at a table for two under the cafe's striped awning. They gazed at each other with unsubtle smiles as raindrops tapped above them and dropped like crystals on the sidewalk.

Order anything on the menu that you want, Jim said—or thought he said—in Spanish.

Order everything? Diego repeated. He heard Americans were notoriously glutinous but "everything on the menu" seemed unbelievable. Hungry as he was, he couldn't believe his luck.

When the waiter arrived, eyebrow already raised, Diego ordered everything on the menu.

"Todo en el menú?" asked the waiter. He looked at Jim, who was too absorbed in Diego to pay attention.

"Si, si!" Jim answered, waving the waiter away. It wasn't until eight cups and six glasses of various beverages and the contents of the dessert tray were laid out on their table that Jim discovered their bilingual game of telephone.

Jim's Ivy League alma mater assisted Diego in getting a student visa. Within weeks they settled together in Jim's townhouse on Jane Street.

Diego and Jim practiced English as often as they could. Diego had every intention of attending school, but the lure of the city was too magnetic, more magnificent than his crumbling guidebook could ever convey.

Diego had every intention of getting his visa taken care of, but the cocoon of Greenwich Village kept real world concerns at bay, and it expired on the first day of 1970.

On March 8th of that year, Jim left for another business trip. The following Saturday night, Diego and a bunch of his friends, already giddy from a birthday party, decided to hit the Snake Pit on West 10th Street for a nightcap.

It was eight months after the Stonewall riots, yet the police continued to harass bars around the neighborhood. That night, they rounded up 163 patrons in the dark basement of the Snake Pit (Diego and his friends included) and marched them down to the 6th precinct.

Diego panicked. He wasn't worried about being harassed for being gay. He was more concerned about his expired visa. Once they found out about his status, they'd send him back to Argentina, and he'd never see Jim again.

The police made the Snake Pit patrons stand in a single file line in the second floor hallway of the 6th precinct building until the sun began to rise. Diego saw its pinkish light through a smoky, cracked window across from him. He noticed the window was open, and the only thing that kept him from jumping to his escape was a flimsy, rusted screen.

Diego counted to ten and made a beeline for the window. He threw open the sash and punched out the screen. He though he could take a second story jump without much trouble, but he never anticipated the spiked metal railing below.

When Jim returned a week later, he rushed to St. Vincent's where Diego lay in a coma. Major organs had been punctured, numerous arteries severed, a pair of his lower vertebrae pushed clean out his skin. He was not expected to live. If, by chance, he did survive, his body would never function properly and complex surgeries would be commonplace.

Despite his condition, Diego was still a beautiful sight to behold. Jim held his hand and whispered bad Spanish into his ear. He told Diego he would never give up on him. Jim had no familial ties to Diego, yet the nurses allowed him to sit by Diego's bedside without question. Many nights the nurses brought in a cot for Jim.

There were a few stories about Diego in the press and even discussions of martyrdom among the most zealous gay rights organizers. Upstart activists said the police had pushed Diego from the second floor window of the 6th precinct. It was time to push back!

Jim had missed the large candlelight vigil for Diego outside St. Vincent's. Since his return, he was approached by well-wishers and hardliners who pleaded with him to join their cause and fight back for the sake of his boyfriend. But Jim was a businessman; he dealt in commodities and monetary value, not human rights and civilian-reviewed police boards. Jim held a corporate position forged with his sweat and blood; he was certainly not ready to destroy all of that by coming out of the closet. Jim's lack of courage and fear of losing everything did not mean he did not love Diego. It's just the way things were.

After 17 days in the ICU, Diego opened his eyes. Everything was beige. Something beeped. Jim slept in a chair to the right, snoring, chin on his chest. He had been reading a book—*Time and Again* by Jack Finney—and it straddled his left thigh.

"Te amo, Jim," Diego said, but it came out like a whisper. His chest hurt and his lungs felt compressed. He took a gentle breath, winced, and tried again. "Te amo, Jimmy!"

Jim dreamt that Diego was saying, I love you, in Spanish, very softly. He smiled in his sleep.

Diego took another painful inhale and tried his best to shout, "Yo, idiota! I love you!"

Jim's eyes snapped open. Through all the tubes and the wires, Jim spotted Diego's tawny eyes. His book toppled to the floor as he grabbed Diego's hand. "I love you, Guapo. Te adoro, Hermoso. Tu eres mi todo."

"Todo?" Diego managed a crooked smile. "Todo en el menú?"

For the first time since he and Diego had parted, Jim laughed. "Si, mi amor. Todo."

DUE TO COMPLICATIONS FROM . . .

"Down, down, down into the darkness of the grave
Gently they go, the beautiful, the tender, the kind;
Quietly they go, the intelligent, the witty, the brave.
I know. But I do not approve. And I am not resigned."
—Edna St. Vincent Millay,
Dirge Without Music

AIDS is not a disease. It's a hastily assembled acronym, released in the early days of the pandemic in an attempt to placate the panic, to pin a name on an atrocity that maimed and killed without warning.

The fourth letter stands for "syndrome." The first letter indicates that the syndrome is "acquired." The second and third letters are holdouts from its previous incarnation, "GRID," or "gay related immune deficiency," a slightly better replacement for the initial term, "gay cancer."

Oddly, just the "I" gets a shout-out in "HIV"—as the human immunodeficiency virus has been called since 1984 when a Frenchman and an American negotiated its cross-Atlantic "co-discovery." Confirming what most frontline doctors already assumed, the scientists explained that the virus replicates in white blood cells and distributes itself through the intermingling of bodily fluids, something humans love to do. The virus weakens an infected individual's immune system, making the person susceptible to a checklist of 26 diseases cobbled together by the Centers for Disease Control.

Just before the winter break of my freshman year, a few weeks after our bleak visit to The Saint, Peter took me to see *The Normal Heart* at the Public Theater. It's not that a friend had canceled or he somehow had an extra ticket. This time, he bought the ticket with me in mind. He'd already seen the play and thought I would benefit from its message.

As much as he liked the other AIDS play, *As Is*, up on Broadway, he hoped Larry Kramer's hit would terrify and enrage me. He saw it as a continuation of the conversation he began when we met in Chicago. Now that HIV was the clear culprit and a test could detect antibodies, Peter admitted to coming out of his celibacy and into safe sex, by which he meant he hired hot straight guys (presumably HIV-negative) to blow him.

AIDS and HIV deniers included established doctors and medical researchers. They published volumes questioning one single cause of immunosuppression. They challenged the efficacy—and ethics—of Western medicine itself. One of the best-known specialists early on was Dr. Joseph Sonnabend, who stressed that all infectious diseases were multi-factorial in nature. In 1983, the doctor lost the lease on his 12th Street office across from St. Vincent's because tenants in his building didn't like that he treated so many AIDS patients.

Pinning the myriad ways AIDS affected people on a solitary virus seemed too easy. HIV was a correlation— not the causation—of morbidity. AZT was poison. Promiscuity itself led to lower protective CD-4 cells. A deficient immune system could be boosted with proper nutrition and a host of tinctures, teas, and 10-K runs. Switch to a macrobiotic diet. Exercise excessively. Question everything: Why did some infected people get sick while others remained vibrant? How is it some gay men tested negative for HIV antibodies but died of AIDS-related causes? Why did the virus—if there was such a thing—target marginalized communities? Why now?

The New York Native, a biweekly gay newspaper operated by the same man who published *Opera News*, printed theories of every stripe. Each week's issue cited a new cause, reported on new culprits. Their unwavering position on African Swine Fever as the root cause of AIDS eventually put them out of existence.

By 1990, a reported 139,765 people in the United States were infected with HIV. Their mortality rate was 60%. That April, Ryan White died. Meanwhile, a group of scientists claimed to trace the first known case of AIDS to a man who died in 1959.

In June, a poll conducted by *The New York Times* and WCBS-TV revealed that 29% of black respondents believed it "true" or "might possibly be true" that HIV "was deliberately created in a laboratory in order to infect black people."

At a press conference in November the following year, 32-year-old point guard for the Lakers "Magic" Johnson announced his seropositive status, and the public face of AIDS morphed yet again. Doctors and scientists released data about AIDS at breakneck speed. People with HIV swam through information and dispensed it to others, but the public only grew more frightened. Sex was dangerous. Blood was a killer. No one was truly safe. By 1994, 41,669 United States citizens were dead due to complications from AIDS.

Aside from the common use of recreational drugs and alcohol, rampant low self-esteem, and the lack of healthy living habits, I imagined that a new and different infectious agent might bear some as-yet-unknown responsibility for someone's decline. Something like a prion, which I'd read was the name of the thing that caused Mad Cow's disease, living co-dependently with the virus like cowbirds flitting about a herd of hairy, but harmless, bison. The detection of HIV antibodies in my blood did not mean I was going to die a horrible death from AIDS. Per se. The detection of HIV antibodies indicated that there might be possible trouble down the road. Things might get hairy. Or so I told myself with a denial that rivaled my mother's.

Until 1996, an HIV-positive diagnosis meant swift and certain death. And it wasn't just one virus, it turned out, as researchers continued to toss confusing research on the HIV bonfire. Two types, HIV-1 and HIV-2, were announced, as were a variety of strains and groups and subtypes. Sometimes, viruses of different subtypes combine within an infected individual to create a "hybrid virus."

Other times, the intermingling of multiple strains can result in "CRFs," circulating recombinant forms—not to be confused with "superinfections" that push immune systems into overdrive as they struggle to respond.

Most scientists believe the original strain of the virus came from infected monkey "bush meat" consumed in the Congo as far back as the 1920s, a "zoonotic pandemic" decades in the making.

Being HIV-positive is a confirmation that HIV antibodies have been activated; it does not mean that person has—or will have—AIDS. Detectable antibodies in the bloodstream are spirits of the brave cells lost as they waged battle against the virus. Before labs could measure the amount of virus in a person's blood, the Center for Disease Control ("CDC") created a somewhat arbitrary baseline of 200 CD4+ T-lymphocytes ("T-cells") to distinguish immuno-decline.

Those with less than 200 T-cells were told to make

end-of-life plans. At one time, I had two remaining T-cells. As the doctor from the Community Health Project informed me, I was "certain to die a horrible death."

Back when Ken was diagnosed, doctors referred to the initial stage of symptoms as "ARC," or "AIDS-related complex," a term used to distinguish the increasingly gray area between those who were merely AIDS-y from those with full-blown AIDS and those with no symptoms at all. Many of us used ARC as a shorthand excuse to slow down our lives, take care of ourselves, and collect disability.

I decided to live out the remainder of my days on the dole. Actually, it was less a decision than my only option. I needed insurance. Two T-cells, destitution, and few hyped-up symptoms would get me Medicaid.

I quit my job at the restaurant—I didn't want to carry plates to my grave anyway—and bled my bank account closed, which wasn't very hard to do. With the assistance of a social worker, I received Social Security disability, health insurance, monthly payments of about $400, and rent assistance from the City's Division of AIDS Services.

I didn't look sick. To the naked eye and without my medical paperwork handy, a stranger might venture to say I was fine. But it wasn't for me, or a stranger, to say that I had AIDS.

I was still clinging to Abbott and Costello, but low T-cell count alone didn't qualify me for "full-blown AIDS," according to the CDC classification system. That determination would only be made if I also contracted one or more of the following conditions: candidiasis of the bronchi, trachea, lungs, or esophagus, cervical cancer, coccidioidomycosis, cryptococcosis, cryptosporidiosis, cytomegalovirus and cytomegalovirus retinitis, encephalopathy, herpes simplex, histoplasmosis, isosporiasis, Kaposi sarcoma, Burkitt's lymphoma, immunoblastic lymphoma, brain lymphoma, mycobacterium avium complex, mycobacterium (not from birds), mycobacterium tuberculosis (both pulmonary and extra-pulmonary, and presumably not from birds), pneumocystis carnii pneumonia, progressive multifocal leukoencephalopathy, recurrent salmonella septicimia, toxoplasmosis of the brain, tuberculosis, wasting, recurrent pneumonia, and the boogie-woogie blues.

Aside from a few Soviet scientists, research on T-cells in the general populace before AIDS came along was scarce. In the early days of the pandemic, frontline doctors sent blood samples from their infected patients to the University of Nebraska, the only place with the technological means to test for T-cells. The CDC eventually declared that the reference interval of CD4+ T-lymphocytes in humans with "healthy" immune systems should range anywhere between 200 and 1,000 per microliter of blood.

Once T-cells fell below the 200-mark, went the oft-told tale, the immune system grew more and more helpless. Any day of the week, the symptoms for any number of ungodly afflictions, real or imagined, might arise. And no case was the same for every person. Because it seemed so hopeless and random, we fixated on things we could measure: the presence of viral antibodies, the latest T-cell count, the number of people infected or dead. And because deaths came quickly and the names of the diseases that caused those deaths were so complicated, it was easier for anchormen and obit writers to say So-and-So "died due to complications from AIDS" and call it a day.

AIDS meant red ribbons on shiny lapels at awards shows, healthy actors starving themselves to win Oscars, Elizabeth Taylor, Princess Diana, and Elton John.

AIDS meant candlelit vigils, teddy bears, balloon shrines, angel iconography, an expansive quilt on the National Mall.

AIDS meant Silence=Death, upside down triangles, Reagan as Hitler, a second holocaust.

AIDS meant another episode of "us versus them" in the long history of our contentiousness. Not even the trinity of a white boy from Indiana, the "people's princess," and an all-star NBA millionaire could alter the prevailing attitude that AIDS was a gay man's burden.

In the marginalia of my sporadic journals, a morbid timeline records the progression. As I noted the deaths of my cultural heroes, I forged an outline of the devastation. I was too young to know the dying on the 7th floor at St. Vincent's, but I was aware of the deaths that grabbed headlines. Like the mass exodus from the closet that preceded the plague years, the profusion of bold-faced gay men dying from AIDS opened the eyes of the world.

On January 15, 1987, I wrote, "Sam Wagstaff, rich collector & Mapplethorpe's lover, dead." On February 5, 1987, I scoffed, "Liberace!! Watermelon diet, my ass!"

On April 17, 1987, I noted the passing of Willi Smith, whose two-toned clothes I wanted to wear but couldn't afford. Charles Ludlam, founder of the Ridiculous Theater Company, took his final bow on May 28, followed two months later by Michael Bennett, the man behind *A Chorus Line* and *Dreamgirls*. In September, underground film director Jack Smith died, followed by photographer Peter Hujar around Thanksgiving.

After enduring a Sandra Bernhard "holiday" show on a visit to Chicago (December 16, 1988), I wrote, "before she belted out her screechy rendition of *Mighty Real*, she told us that Sylvester had died earlier that day in San Francisco. She had that palpable excitement bearers of death scoops get. I found no consolation in her upraised fist and her demand that we, the audience, 'Fight AIDS!' The evening was ruined."

On March 10, 1989, I noted Mapplethorpe's death. No surprise—his deterioration had been widely publicized. That summer, Steve Rubell died, the man who created Studio 54, the beacon that brought me to New York City. In December, choreographer Alvin Ailey and writer and *Female Trouble* star Cookie Mueller followed.

The 1990s began with the demise of designer Patrick Kelly, "reportedly the result of a brain tumor and bone marrow disease, according to his obit. He was 35."

On February 16, I wrote three words: "Keith Haring! Fuck!" Keith had been an approachable icon. His chalk drawings graced the subway when I came to the city.

In quick succession, nearly once a month, dead heroes filled my journal: Halston, John Sex, Vito Russo, Howard Ashman, Brad Davis, Freddie Mercury, Robert Reed, David Wojnarowicz, Al Parker, Anthony Perkins, Rudolf Nureyev, Randy Shilts, Derek Jarman, Marlon Riggs, John Preston, John Boswell, Leigh Bowery.

I recorded Bobby's passing during the early morning hours of February 2, 1995. Eight days later, the death of Paul Monette, a man who wrote so bravely and truthfully about the death of his long-time partner in *Borrowed Time*, became a sort of punctuation mark for my timeline. It was too overwhelming to grasp. By 1995, 50,877 Americans had lost their lives due to complications from HIV/AIDS related causes.

Six months after Bobby's death, I had trouble swallowing. Whenever I ate, I had to have water nearby. Without it, choking down small bites of food felt like swallowing gravel. As my discomfort increased, my appetite decreased. By October, even the softest, blandest foods caused stabbing pains that began in my throat before radiating to the center of my chest. I knew it might be something serious. I hoped by ignoring it, it would go away. But when a sip of water had me doubling over and wincing, I decided it was time to get some answers.

I could no longer afford to see Dr. Braun. At what

ended up being my final appointment, his front desk minions informed me that the good doctor didn't accept Medicaid. The receptionist suggested I visit the HIV Clinic at St. Vincent's in the ground floor of the O'Toole Building. She handed me a slip of paper with the phone number.

"You might want to call right away to schedule an appointment, they're always booked," she said.

In the meantime, she added, Dr. Braun was kind enough to refer me to the main hospital to get an endoscopy "to get the ball rolling" for whoever picked up my case. I called the clinic when I got home and made an appointment for the morning of October 31. Halloween was the last thing on my mind.

The official name for the whimsical structure on Seventh Avenue, between West 12th and West 13th Streets, was The Edward and Theresa O'Toole Medical Services Building, named after a couple who made a fortune selling religious goods, but everyone called it the "Overbite" because its cantilevered floors of white tiles resemble asymmetrical jaws with wavy teeth.

In the early 1960s, one of its original residents called it "the box in which the Guggenheim Museum came." Designed by Albert C. Ledner for the National Maritime Union of America, St. Vincent's gave it a new life in 1973. If sluggish elevators, outdated equipment, and a collective disgruntlement that permeated the labyrinthine hallways and wood-paneled offices can be called "new life."

Gray plastic netting, stretched across every scalloped

gap, did nothing to prevent pigeons from nested between the Overbite's teeth. Tall metal fencing surrounded the ground floor to prevent vagrants from using it as a campground. It served as a large ashtray and garbage receptacle for the hundreds of patients that came in and out all day—as well as all the thousands of commuters going into or getting out of the 2 and 3 subway train entrance at the building's southeast corner.

Scratched glass doors were manned by disinterested security guards. When opened, the din of children and even louder adults emerged like a gust of wind. Unattended children in Princess Jasmine and Teen-Age Mutant Ninja Turtle costumes gorged themselves on the hard candy heaped in bowls on the reception desks.

A woman in cat ears at the front desk flirted with a security guard with devil horns on his bald head. I told her I had an appointment. She snickered when I said I was a little early. She checked my Medicaid card and my driver's license, then gave me a clipboard of paperwork to fill out. She assigned me a number, color-coded to match my HIV-status, and told me to sit in the area marked "Communicative and Infectious Diseases."

The paperwork took 10 minutes. I read it over again and double-checked my answers as if I had finished early on an exam. I didn't think to bring anything to read, so I stared at the floor for about 45 minutes until my number was called. A woman in blue scrubs led me to a small examining room. Its cleanliness—and the sunlight streaming through the window—caught me by surprise.

"Take off your clothes," said the woman in blue scrubs. "You can keep your underwear on." She tossed me a threadbare white gown. "And put this on. Front or back, doesn't matter."

She left the room and closed the door. I assumed she was a nurse. Maybe she was the doctor. Maybe it was a costume. She had a nametag on, and I reminded myself to read it when she returned, but I never saw her again.

I hung my clothes on a hook behind the door. I'd gone commando for the day, so I tied the gown snugly around my waist. I sat on the examining table and watched the clock. Another half hour passed until a slip of a man with a comb-over, overgrown eyebrows, and a gnarly grey mustache burst through the door. Under his food-stained lab coat, I noticed a mustard plaid polyester jacket, a purple paisley shirt with enormous collars, and a wide brown tie. His nametag said, "Ross Zorvos, MD." He greeted me with a firm handshake and an awkward enthusiasm. "I'm Dr. Ross."

He made a show of washing his hands, then turned to me and smiled. "What seems to be the problem?" There was something green in his teeth.

I told him I was having a hard time swallowing. I told him eating was impossible, that I had lost about fifteen pounds, and it was only getting worse. He looked over my chart. I imagined all of my information arriving in the bowels of the Overbite through a pneumatic tube connected to the front desk at Dr. Braun's office.

"You have AIDS," the doctor said, as if this were a

105

revelation.

"Well," I said as he grabbed for my throat, "I'm HIV-positive."

He hoisted me up by my armpits. "Your nodes aren't that swollen." He seemed disappointed.

"Did you get the results from my endoscopy?"

"They're not in your chart. Who performed it?"

"Excuse me?"

"Who performed your endoscopy?"

"Dr. Braun ordered it. Over at St. Vincent's, the Raskob Building, a few days ago. I don't remember the name of the guy who did it."

Dr. Ross grabbed the wall phone; buttons flashed like Christmas lights. "Let me see if I can call over there." He fiddled a bit before a woman's voice escaped the earpiece: "Hello?"

"Hi. I'm trying to call over to the GI unit."

"Well, honey, that ain't me." Click.

Dr. Ross hung up the phone. He pet his mustache with his fingertips. "Let me check outside. I'll be a minute."

In the silence of the additional minutes, I thought of grabbing my clothes and my medical chart. But there was nowhere else to go.

Dr. Ross reappeared, victorious, the results of my endoscopy raised above his head. He showed still-frame color images of the swollen red hole in the pink lining of my esophagus. "It's quite an ulcer," he said. "It's why you can't swallow."

He pointed a chewed pencil at the images and continued, "It's about a half-an-inch wide. Could be a number of things. Let's bring you in and do some tests. We'll get you hooked up to some nourishment, get your strength back. Figure out what this thing is."

He checked his watch. He looked at my chart. His brows arched. "You don't live too far from here. Well, they start closing down 6th Avenue at 5:30 for the parade, so you may want to get home and grab a few things, then get back here to the ER as quickly as you can."

"The ER?" Everything was happening so quickly. I wasn't ready for the 7th floor.

"Yes, I'll let them know I'll be admitting you."

I hustled back to the apartment and tried to decide what "few things" I needed for an undefined length of time in the hospital. I grabbed my toothbrush, toothpaste, contact lens stuff, shampoo, conditioner. I wanted to pretend I was going on vacation. I grabbed a pair of sweatpants and my slippers and the terry cloth robe that Bobby had given me for Christmas. I stuffed everything in a green and white New York Jets duffel bag that had once belonged to Stewart.

I made my way to 7th Avenue. Through a phalanx of wicked witches and Spice Girls, Trekkies and Stormtroopers, zombies and old fashioned ghosts, I made my way to the ER of St. Vincent's for the third time in a decade.

It had been more than three years since I welcomed the New Year with a burning strep throat and godawful morning television. It had been more than five years since I'd jumped from the Highline and busted my ankle. Just a year ago, Bobby and I were about to leave for Key West.

Dr. Ross didn't show up until the following morning. He left word with the ER staff to admit me to the 7th floor once a bed opened up. They rushed about briskly, politely, pleasant without committing to cheer. The women touched my shoulder and called me "baby" and asked extraneous questions. Couldn't Dr. Ross answer their questions? Wasn't it all in my patient file?

"I'm in excruciating pain, I have not eaten for weeks and I'd love it if you'd knock me out," I told them, but a couple of Tylenols and a rectal exam were all they able to provide.

I passed in and out of consciousness until 1 in the morning when a masked orderly wheeled me to the elevator to take me to the 7th floor. I was greeted by a nurse named Kathy. A Midwest girl, my guess. Perhaps upstate. She was wholesome-looking and battle-tested and, God bless her, quick to bring a syringe with 2 mg of Dilaudid once I was situated in my new bed.

She then stuck a tube into the crook of my elbow that was connected to a jar of thick, white liquid she called a "milkshake." She assured me it would pump nutrition into my veins.

I was in a semi-private room, split by a curtain that obscured the window and all but the foot of my silent roommate's bed. Kathy confirmed that he was catatonic.

"How are we doing, Walter?" she shouted out.

No answer. Seven floors below, Halloween revelers made their way through the streets, the bass from boom boxes thundered alongside shrieks of drunken laughter.

Kathy shook her head and lowered her voice. "Sometimes he makes strange noises. He's in a lot of pain, we know that. No visitors, poor guy. Well, good night!" She tugged the beige and cream striped curtain that surrounded my bed and disappeared.

I was alone. I was sick. But I wasn't scared. I was high. High enough to forget my burning chest and my growling stomach. High enough to drift in and out of sleep. High enough to think the sporadic moans coming from Walter were those of pleasure. High enough to think Dr. Ross would figure out what was wrong with me and fix it.

A ST. VINNY'S XMAS FANTASIA: 1983

"I think Ed Koch is the person most responsible for allowing AIDS
to get out of control. It happened here first, on his watch. If he had done what
any moral human being should have done in the beginning, and put out alarms,
then a lot fewer people would have gotten sick."

—Larry Kramer

"And I feel like I'm gonna' die
I don't feel so good inside
Why baby, why, why, why?
But I had a good time
You know I had a good night."

—The Ramones,
"Death of Me"

"How'm I doin', Doc?!" asked the patient, squinting, grinning, bald. Only partially joking. He thought for sure he'd met his Maker just an hour before, but now he felt just fine. A little foolish. A little angry that he wasn't brought to Beth Israel. "What's your name? You look like a college kid!"

The bright-eyed doctor smiled and held out his hand. His nametag read "Dr. Razi. The mayor of New York was his first celebrity patient. "You're going to be fine, Mr. Mayor. Just breathe. We'll have you up and out of here in no time."

Poinsettias lined the ER waiting room. Red and green tinsel hung from the triage hallway. A weathered Santa cutout graced the exit door. The inescapable chug-chug-chug of "Billie Jean" echoed down the corridor from a nurse's radio.

The mayor watched his companion, wrapped in a black fur, as she moved between his men like a boozy bear in heels.

"Where is this, St. Vinny's? I asked to be taken to Beth Israel."

"No, you did not, Ed. Now, shush and let the doctor do his job."

"He looks like a kid, Bess."

Bess slapped her friend's shiny head. "Ed, he can hear you."

The mayor was suddenly lethargic. "How'm I doin'?" he slurred.

Bess smiled wanly.

Dr. Razi asked for a nurse to wheel the mayor away to make room for the night's influx: a few of the neighborhood's walking dead, years beyond their ages, raised lesions on hollow faces, gasping for oxygen, waiting to be admitted; a fifteen-year-old stabbed near the West 4th Street basketball court; a couple of drunken

111

NYU students hit by a delivery truck on Greenwich Avenue; another co-ed OD; an old woman from the produce aisle at Balducci's diagnosed her own broken hip and asked if anyone knew a good lawyer. And now, the 105th Mayor of New York City.

Dr. Razi turned to Bess. "Has Mr. Koch been drinking excessively this evening?"

Bess laughed. It was clear to the doctor that she had been. "No more than usual," she answered. "I think it's his stress level. Burns his candle at both ends. Between you and I, Dr.—er, Razi? What is that?"

"My parents are Persian."

"Oh, the Persians!" She shook her head and sighed ecstatically. "But you know about the Persians." She touched the hairs of the doctor's short beard with her upturned fingernails.

"You think that he's been working too hard?"

"Always. Between you and I, Dr. Razi," she whispered conspiratorially, "he's not been the same since his loss to Cuomo. He really wanted the governorship, you know? And he would have been damned good in Albany! He's a good man, Dr. Razi." She made a sweep of the room with her nose in the air. "Don't let any one tell you otherwise."

"Can we get you a cup of coffee, Mrs.--?"

"Myerson," she answered coyly. There was no recognition his eyes. "Bess Myerson." Still nothing. "Just call me Bess. Will this be long, Doctor? He really only fainted. Pansies do that all the time." She elbowed

Dr. Razi in the ribs as if they were onstage doing vaudeville.

"We just need to run some tests before we can release him. Why don't you get some coffee and check back in about a half hour?"

Bess gazed at her Cartier watch. "Almost midnight! Chri'ma'nutleys!" She patted the doctor's shoulder. "Where would we be without friends?"

Dr. Razi shrugged, smiled, and took a step back.

Bess approached a couple of suits gathered near the door. "Oh, boys," she purred. "Stay with Hizzoner, would you? Tell him I'll call the cleaning lady."

Bess's perfume lingered long after she had left.

A runaway youth named Sammy occupied Dr. Razi next. He'd been sent over with a chaperone from the Covenant House. Sore throat for the past few days, vomiting every half hour since the afternoon. His arms were riddled with track marks.

Dr. Razi filled out another set of forms, then asked the nurse to line him up behind the mayor and before the lady with the broken hip.

"Maybe just a nosh!" the mayor bellowed. "My blood sugar's low. I just need a little something to eat." One of the suits wrestled with a handful of singles as he ambled off to the candy machine.

An incoming siren silenced the hallway.

"We got a serious head injury!"

An EMT wheeled in what appeared to be a bloody rumple of shredded black clothing. Dr. Razi took a closer

113

look. The patient's head had been bashed in with a beer bottle. Bits of green glass stuck out at all angles from his red, matted hair. Upon further inspection, the doctor spotted a small crack in the skull through which he could see the kid's brain. His eyes were fixed, the pupils large.

"We're going to need an operating room. Is Dr. Fahey on duty? Let's get this man up to surgery." Dr. Razi leaned in to the patient. "We're going to fix you up, young man. Stay strong."

The orderlies whisked the gurney to the elevators.

Sammy, the kid from Covenant House, was suddenly animated. "Oh my God! That's Johnny Ramone!!" He raised his arm and pumped his fist. His i.v. tube flailed like a jump rope. "Gabba gabba hey, dude!"

There was no response from Johnny.

"Gabba gabba heyyyyyyy," Sammy shouted again as the elevator doors slid shut.

Dr. Razi had a punk roommate at Cornell who exposed him to all of the American madness his parents had shielded him from. Including the Ramones. They may not have been Dr. Razi's favorite band, but they held a special place in his Persian-American heart. Adrenaline raced through Dr. Razi's bloodstream. Two celebrities in one night!

At around 1:30, after looking over the mayor's preliminary numbers, Dr. Razi told him, "You're fine on paper and free to go. Your blood pressure is a little high, but I suspect you know that."

"Without high blood pressure and, I suppose, ego,

I would deflate, Doctor." The mayor stood gently, a suit on either side for balance.

"I'm good. I'm good!" He pushed the men away to mime a soft shoe. "Thanks to the good Doctor Razi here. Well, I have a crazy week ahead of me. Can we go?"

The doctor nodded. "Happy Hanukkah, Mr. Mayor."

"Happy Holidays, Doctor Razi!"

The suits led the mayor through the reception area ablaze with gaudy red bows. A crew of filthy punks with teased-up hair were scattered like lazy vermin across the room. Ripped clothing the color of cigar ash, steel-toed engineer boots, ratty brown denim, sunken, sleepy, blood-shot eyes: no-good punks, thought the mayor. One of the many scourges of his administration. What these guys needed was a good war. Clean them right up. Give them purpose.

Serving in World War II was the best thing that ever happened to the mayor. He'd heard the same from lawyers who'd served in Vietnam. As a self-proclaimed "liberal with sanity," these torn young men and the dirty, misguided girl with them made the mayor feel hopeless.

A lanky member of the bunch stood and approached. "Mr. Mayor," the hoodlum said. The mayor jumped. The suits formed a wedge.

"How'ya'doin'?" the mayor answered, hoping to alleviate any tension.

"Your honor," said the punk, stepping over a man sleeping on the floor. "May I shake your hand?"

Hizzoner winced.

"You don't know me, but you were good to my family."

The mayor pushed the suits aside and extended his hand. "What's your name?"

"Joey Ramone. Real name's Jeffrey Hyman. You helped my dad and his buddies keep the projects out of Forest Hills back in '73."

Ah, yes. That monstrosity of Lindsay's. Was he insane? An enormous low-income housing project smack dab in the middle of middle-class Queens? The mayor fondly recalled his counter-move to doom the project. It put him on the map and helped him beat that dago in '77.

"Vote for Cuomo, Not the Homo," indeed. Made me the most powerful mayor on earth. Let Mario live in godforsaken Albany.

"Great to meet you, Joey," the mayor said. "Glad I could be of help."

The handshake went on too long, but neither could seem to let go.

The mayor pretended he could see his idling limo through the glass doors. "Ah, my car. Good luck to your brother in there."

"He's not my brother, but thanks. It seems we all end up in this place at some point."

The mayor nodded absentmindedly. "Well, good night, Joey."

"Merry Christmas, Mr. Mayor."

TANGIBLE WEIGHT

"They carried all the emotional baggage of men who might die.
Grief, terror, love, longing—these were intangibles, but the intangibles
had their own mass and specific gravity, they had tangible weight."
—Tim O'Brien,
The Things They Carried

That winter Dr. Ross and the good people at St. Vincent's kept Demarol and Dilaudid flowing through my veins as they ran various tests, drew blood daily, performed three endoscopies, and eventually inserted a Port-a-cath just above my heart.

Instead of trying to find the simplest solution to the cause and treatment of the ulcers in my esophagus—as if I were any other patient—Dr. Ross and company saw the H, I, and V on my chart and assumed the worst. A few days before Thanksgiving he diagnosed me with cytomegalovirus (in its inevitable shorthand, CMV), one of the CDC's Top 26 opportunistic infections.

"CMV is a relatively harmless virus for those with healthy immune systems," the doctor informed me. "It's mostly found in the eye and tends to cause blindness. It's also known to cause damage to the esophagus. In fact, most people in their lifetimes encounter the virus but never suffer complications. We are seeing what it can do when unleashed in an immuno-compromised host."

They implanted the aforementioned port catheter so I could administer a refrigerated dose of Ganciclovir intravenously every twelve hours. It looked like a small plastic knob stuck to my left upper pectoral.

Ganciclovir was a newly authorized anti-viral medication made expressly to fight CMV. Although being released from the hospital to treat myself seemed scary, it was a series of encouraging steps.

A nurse demonstrated how to keep the open wound in my chest clean every time I peeled away the dressing to give myself the medicine. She showed me how to apply sterile dressing with disposable latex gloves. She warned about infections if I wasn't diligent or if I got sloppy. She listed adverse reactions I might experience. Without irony, she told me it would inhibit my sperm production, then handed me a palm-sized 20-page accordion of paper to peruse at home.

The drug itself came as a liquid in small latex dispenser balls with needles that plugged into the catheter burrowed into my chest. In the course of about an hour, the drug oozed down into my superior vena cava and spread, still cold, through my bloodstream. The feeling freaked me out at first, but eventually I got used to it.

On the morning I was first released, an early snowfall brought the streets of the Village to a whitewash hush. My friend Kevin took the Jets duffle bag I'd inherited from Stewart. I packed up all the crap visitors had brought into a plastic bag that read: "Belongings of ..." with blank lines for a name and an address like a postcard.

Dr. Ross shook my hand and wished me luck. I said goodbye to the nurses. They handed me a prescription for Oxycodone. The pills were meant to manage the pain when I ate, yet they were impossible to swallow.

I descended in the elevator to the lobby. I read and re-read the sign on the doors: "Discretion is a virtue. Don't talk about patients in the elevator." I felt like an inmate on parole, frightened to move toward the exit, to get myself home, to survive.

Chilled to the core, I took a cab to East 10th Street, to Bobby's penthouse. To pay the rent while I wasted away, Kevin and Chiclet had moved in. Chiclet had recently transitioned and now lived as Adriana. Neither was thrilled to have me back from the hospital. Although it was good to have living breathing people around all day and throughout the night instead of visiting hours, I didn't bring much holiday joy in return.

It was supposed to be my apartment, my dream apartment when I was younger and healthier. Now it held too many memories. I could only think about Bobby.

When I was in the hospital, Adriana slept in the master bedroom in Bobby's king-sized bed. We shared it when I returned. Her full, warm body on the mattress beside me brought comfort.

Kevin took the second bedroom, what Bobby called the maid's room, the one I slept in when he was alive. A stuffed blue swordfish on the north wall presided over filing cabinets, boxes, outmoded clothes, and old suitcases. Underneath it all, Kevin found a place to sleep.

My first morning back, I awoke to a violent rapping at the sliding glass doors. Adriana snorted a few inches from my ear. "Not again," she whined.

I stumbled to the window and opened the curtains. In the snowy mist, through the bloodied window, a cardinal shook his head on a bare branch. He raised his wings and struck again. Despite the red streaks on the fogged glass, he attacked his reflection repeatedly.

"My God," Adriana wailed from the bed, startling me even further. "What is wrong with that damned bird?!" She rolled back and forth, entangling her Botero limbs in the sheets. "Every goddamned morning! You'd think it would learn by now!"

I tried to grab some breakfast before my morning dose of Ganciclovir. The cannabis-laced cookies my friend Kathleen brought by to encourage my appetite were slightly helpful, but I still couldn't eat or drink without pain.

After three weeks, a follow-up endoscopy revealed that the holes in my esophagus had not changed since I started the Ganciclovir. I weighed what I did in high school, when I wrestled and starved myself to make the 126-pound weight class.

But what I lost wasn't just measured on a scale. It took a toll on my psyche—and those of my friends and roommates. It destroyed any semblance of ego I had left. I once had broad shoulders and what Kevin called a "lesbian ass." All that hard-earned muscle from years of running and weightlifting evaporated. Like many gay men, I had body dysmorphia. The goal of our physical hard work was to be perfect, to be perceived as healthy and desirable. It was shame that drove us to drink and do drugs and have sex with lots people we didn't know.

When people expressed concern over my diminishing frame, I would joke about wearing one of those LOSE WEIGHT NOW! ASK ME HOW! buttons.

If people asked, for example, "How do you stay so skinny?"

I'd whisper, "AIDS."

"It hasn't gotten worse," Dr. Ross told me after our first appointment since my release. "Let's give it some more time."

Peter called a few days later. He was sorry he hadn't been able to visit. He'd been in Palm Springs looking at properties and had just returned to the city to begin the process of selling his company and perhaps relocate to Los Angeles. He asked if I'd like to join him and a gaggle of yuppie gays for a weekend in DC to see the blockbuster Vermeer show at the National Gallery of Art.

It was the kind of art show Peter could identify with: it was exclusive (hard-to-get tickets), it was extravagant (six round-trip plane tickets and six swanky hotel rooms), it was once-in-a-lifetime (not since Delft in 1696 had so many paintings from the Dutch Master appeared in one place).

I couldn't eat. I was weak and in pain. I had a catheter in my chest that required the nightly feeding of an ice-cold drug that didn't seem to be working. A trip in my condition might have been ill advised, but I needed an escape. Besides, I had nothing to lose.

Turns out, one of Peter's friends was the son of a scientist in charge of the development of the drug I was pumping nightly into my chest. Although it was the last thing I wanted to talk about, Peter sat us together on the plane.

I told the kid I didn't think his father's breakthrough pharmaceutical was as successful with the ulcer in my esophagus as it seemed to be with retinitis, which I'd read had actual results. "Maybe it would be better if I had it in my eye," I added.

The kid wasn't amused. He turned to another of Peter's friends across the aisle and began to discuss how Vermeer used a pin and a string to work out the perspective in his paintings—something they'd both read in *The New Yorker*.

The entire flight had been turbulent, but as we neared Dulles, flashes lit the windows and rumbles shook the air. We'd left behind snow squall in Newark to float in the eye of a mid-Atlantic storm. Outside my window, against slate grey clouds and intermittent blasts of electricity, beads of water stretched like mercury against the glass.

Then the cabin lights cut out, and everything went dark. A bolt of lightning hit the runway, and the pilot aborted the landing. We shot straight back up into the air.

Everyone gripped at whatever was closest, seat rests, tray tables, children, each other, screaming, gasping, praying. I wasn't frightened at all.

The pilot leveled the plane and circled the airport for another approach. Our second attempt at landing was successful. By the time the plane taxied to the gate, Peter and his gaggle were attempting to laugh their terror off, ribbing one another about life insurance claims and Depend undergarments. We all knew how close we had come to death.

We never saw the Vermeer show. By the time we got to the museum, we were told we couldn't get in. We had missed the timed entry on our tickets, and the elderly woman at the velvet rope didn't care that we had almost been killed in a storm to get there.

She peered at the tickets through her reading glasses. "You're nearly two hours late. It's a blockbuster show, you know. I can't just 'let' you in. People come to enjoy the paintings. They don't want to be herded through like sheep." She scanned the six of us. "That's why we have timed entries."

Peter tried to protest.

"There's nothing I can do. Now please move to the

side so I can let the next group in. On time."

Peter reached out to snatch the tickets from the woman's hands. She took a step backward and raised her arms above her head.

"I'd like my tickets back," Peter demanded.

"They're no longer good. Therefore, I must take them."

The kid with the Big Pharma dad stepped forward. "Just give us the tickets."

The woman grabbed a walkie-talkie attached to her waist. "Can I get security at the Vermeer entrance, please?"

I couldn't run, so I straggled behind as Peter's crew skeedaddled their asses down the main stairs of the museum as if their hundred-dollar haircuts were on fire, a much better visual memory than a wing of Vermeers.

That night I opted out of a group dinner at some schmancy place in Georgetown, followed by whatever sad nightlife they could dig up around DuPont Circle. I was unable to get comfortable in my deluxe hotel room, so I sat in the overdone lobby on a purple velvet couch and fed the Port-a-cath under my t-shirt as if I were nursing a baby. Passing guests were suitably horrified. Perhaps that's why I did it.

Three days before Christmas, I was readmitted to the 7th floor. Multi-colored lights and silver lamé bells hung in the hallways. They did little to brighten the dim warren of sickrooms or the ambience of death row.

People told tales of treacherous journeys and perilous

conditions just to get to the hospital. Out the windows, drifts of powder whirled through the quiet streets. A blizzard didn't mean much to us. In the warmth of St. Vincent's, the city below, buried in snow, seemed like another world.

Most patients drew their blinds throughout the day, regardless of the weather. Unlike the curtains that separated patients in our mostly semi-private rooms, our doors remained open. Only visitors closed them.

In the evenings, a stroll through the 7th floor took on the feel of an immersive Nam June Paik installation: black and white 10-inch tv's flickered and flashed in every doorway, machinery blinked, long fluorescents throbbed overhead. Spent bulbs went unchanged for days.

An outside outfit ran the tv rental operation. It cost five bucks a day to watch seven stations: ABC, CBS, NBC, FOX, PBS, and two local channels that mostly played reruns of shows I refused to watch the first time around. Before dinner each night, a woman in a dark blue vest and a fanny pack stuffed with loose change and crumpled singles made her rounds to collect the rent. An unwritten rule prevented her from giving 7th floor patients anything longer than a daily contract until a few repeat admissions convinced her to give us a full week for $25—just as long-term patients on the other floors of the hospital were permitted. Like the angry protests around the country we witnessed on our little rented tv's, the residents of the 7th floor had some victories, too.

Some veterans called the 7th floor, "The Sevens,"

others, "That Fucking Place." It was more of a waiting-room-only hospice than the functioning wing of a hospital. Like the city in microcosm, our beds constituted valuable real estate. We held on to them as long as we could while our immuno-compromised comrades waited downstairs for space to open up. We tried not to get too familiar with one another. The 7th floor was no place to make friends. It wasn't a community. We were all transients.

Visitors may have seen a bunch of zombies propped up in beds staring blankly at bad television, but sleep was not high on the list of 7th floor priorities. There was a constant hum that kept even the comatose restless. The beeping of so many machines echoed like computerized crickets, and throughout the night, nurses went from room to room, answering call buttons and alert signals, administering medication, soothing temperatures, checking buttons and wires, changing tubes and bags. A chorus of grown men moaned in the round and peals of cackling ricocheted through the corridors. Periodic "code blues" pierced the night to remind us what we were up against.

Mornings were announced by a squeaky-wheeled bucket and the slapping and sloshing of a mop on the checkerboard linoleum floors. Around 5:30 am, dark-skinned women in pink scrubs and the most ornate hairstyles came with their carts, taking temperatures, pulse rates, and blood samples as they chatted with one another in high-pitched West Indian patois.

On rare occasions, usually between the serving of breakfast and the start of visiting hours, relative quiet overtook the floor. This was when an assortment of disarmingly cheery volunteers would strike as they weaved their way from doorway to doorway tending to our cultural needs.

A trio of women whose own sons had died due to complications from AIDS pushed tricked-out shopping carts full of books and magazines. On either side were handmade signs that read "LOVE LIBRARIANS."

A volunteer choir also made the rounds once a week. Calling themselves, "Hearts & Voices," the group fluctuated between three and eight people of various ages, genders, and colors, but they sang the same selection of jazz and Broadway standards every visit. Whenever "New York, New York, a helluva' town, the Bronx is up but the Battery's down" began to echo down the hallway, a collective groan would go up. Although Hearts & Voices were pleasant singers and their hearts were in the right place, they were as welcome as colonoscopies. Adriana called them the "Bennetton Jazz Hand Band," and soon everyone else on the floor did too.

Fitting with the overall Catholic theme, the overworked nurses of the 7th floor were Heaven-sent, present, if not immediately available, at all times of the day. Some seemed to be there 24/7. They could have worked in recovery or OB/GYN or even the ER, but in the spirit of the Sisters who founded the hospital in 1849 to battle cholera and tuberculosis and typhoid, the angelic nurses of the 7th floor chose to care for us.

Because most of us couldn't eat, we would kill time in the smoking lounge, certainly the last of its kind in an American hospital. The walls had been sponged by some design queen to give them the look of patinated copper. The couches and chairs had been donated years before. They were oversized, in primary colors, shaped like giant Gumby dolls.

Unattributed quotations were painted in flaking gold letters that ran along the trim of each wall. "OH, SO NOW I SEE, GOD HAS HUMAN EYES," read the one above the door.

Inscribed on the wall beside it, some wishful thinking from the French: "LA VIE EST BELLE ET ELLE COMMENCE DEMAIN."

Fatalistic German, "ALLES GUTE HAT SEIN ENDE," was written on the third wall.

And on the fourth wall, my favorite, "BICHA NAO MORRE, VIRA PURPURINA," which a Brazilian friend translated as "Faggots don't die, they turn to glitter."

There were no proper ashtrays. Styrofoam cups with sips of soda in the bottom were passed around as we sat and smoked and traded acronyms.

"I have PCP and lymph cancer. Last round of chemo nearly killed me."

"I've got KS, MAI, PCP, CMV, and a suspected tumor, to boot. Just had an MRI."

"What do you guys think of AZT?"

"Dumped mine out after the Concorde Study proved

it was bullshit."

"Me, too."

"Me, three. Fuckin' diarrhea pills."

"Poison's what it is. When my lover died, his nightstand was littered with those little amber prescription bottles. It was like a fucking apothecary! He took everything they told him to take and it killed him."

"Bactrim prophylaxis is the only thing worth shit."

"Well, I have CMV retinitis. Now they think there's something in my stomach. I haven't eaten in two weeks and haven't seen the sun in two months."

"I have CMV of the esophagus and haven't eaten in three months," I added. "I can't swallow pills, so I can't take Bactrim." When I mentioned I was taking intravenous Ganciclovir, two guys revealed plastic ports just above their hearts. I showed them mine.

"We're a triptych of bionic gay Jesuses," said one.

"Wouldn't that be Jesii?" posed the other.

We exhaled blue tendrils of smoke as we laughed. Give the dying their vices. What our doctors or the New York City Department of Health could not understand, the angels posing as 7th floor nurses did. They respected our need to experience the sublime release of a cigarette at a time when everything was hopeless. They could not make us well. They could not give us back our looks, our autonomy, our dignity, our privacy. They couldn't guarantee visits from friends or family. They couldn't take the place of absent mothers or dead lovers. They were helpless to solve the pandemic and knew nothing could

129

prevent our impending deaths, so the angels let us smoke because they knew relief's hard to come by during wartime.

In lieu of food or flowers or invites to parties we would not be attending, visitors to the 7th floor—those of us lucky enough to have visitors—brought gossip, books, and weed. The windows in our rooms didn't open, so when we wanted to smoke pot, we'd lock ourselves in the bathroom, place rolled-up towels along the base of the door and exhale into dryer sheets wrapped in another towel. In a cloud of Lysol fumes and dank smoke, we'd emerge giggly as schoolchildren. Of course the nurses knew. Some snickered, others offered half-assed warnings. All of them had more important matters to attend to.

As sick as I got, each day was a parade of visitors. Over the course of my deathwatch came Gregg and Andre and Kevin and Lucy and Mike and Annie and Andrea up from D.C., and my college roommate, Matt, with his latest girlfriend, and Larry, who alluded to my situation in a dance he was choreographing, and Peter, when he was back from LA, and Timmy, when he wasn't taking a beach vacation, and Claudia and Bruce and Josiah and Antonio and James and his boyfriend, Ricardo, who never liked me until I was skeletal and near-death, and Andy in his wheelchair and David and Kathleen, and JoJo, who liked to decorate my room with pictures of himself dressed as rock gods, and Robin and Anna, who brought me copies of *Leaves of Grass* and *The Immoralist* and really good weed.

I especially looked forward to visits from Adriana, the artist formerly known as Chiclet. Her visits were like a twisted Christmas. Not just for me, others on the floor looked forward to her appearances.

Once or twice week she'd arrive, her cello-shaped figure dolled up, carrying my mail and some sheet music in a bright-yellow fake fur satchel. At the off-key upright in the 7th floor rec room, Adriana would play songs by Rachmaninoff and Tchaikovsky and Schopin, some from her warped memory, others from sheet music with pages she'd rip through with dramatic tension.

Adriana liked to improvise for us on occasion. She liked to mash up the John Williams songbook, mixing the sinister opening notes from *Jaws* and her own disconcerting screams into an overly mournful playing of the *Theme from Schindler's List*. It was just the kind of gallows humor we needed. Visitors like Adriana kept our spirits alive. They didn't come by to cry or commiserate or cheer us up. They brought joy without the schmaltz, unlike the Bennetton Jazz Hand Band.

One evening, wandering the halls with my i.v. pole, I saw Dr. Braun at the nurses' station. He was looking over patient charts as he shook snow onto the long, white, counter-size desk. I hadn't seen him since his receptionist suggested I seek medical care at the Overbite.

I called out his name. He looked at me blankly. I introduced myself. My name didn't register. When I mentioned Bobby, his eyes widened. "Oh, yes. You! How are you?"

He didn't ask it like a concerned physician. It was as if he was making small talk at a cocktail party. I opened my robe.

"Port-a-cath," he mouthed. He moved closer to examine it. "You've lost a lot of weight."

"CMV in my esophagus. This is for Ganciclovir."

"How's it working?"

I told him it wasn't. Things had worsened since I first approached him in September with my initial trouble swallowing—before he threw me onto Dr. Ross's caseload.

"Well," he said, jostling folders back and forth. "I've got a number of patients to visit." His scarf dripped like a wet stole.

The next day, Dr. Ross entered my room, leafing through my growing chart desperately. "Well, I'm at odds with what to do next," he said.

In the time it took me to shrug, for I had no other response, Dr. Ross announced that he and Mrs. Dr. Ross would be leaving for Vietnam to celebrate the New Year.

"Have a good time," was all I could muster before turning back to watch Suzanne Somers hawk her ThighMaster. I don't remember if Dr. Ross said goodbye. I certainly didn't care.

I felt a bit differently about my mother's plans for the New Year. As a proud alumnus of Northwestern University, she rooted obsessively for the "Cats," short for "Wildcats," their football team. That season had been unexpectedly excellent; they were chosen to play the Rose Bowl on New Year's Day. There was never a question if she and her husband and some old college friends would travel to Pasadena for the big game.

Phone calls between us were often cloak and dagger affairs. When I called from St. Vincent's, she'd give exaggerated one-word answers to my questions to signify that her husband was in the room, and she couldn't speak freely. Accordingly, we kept in touch through the mail.

Her letters, in beautiful English teacher cursive, concluded with flourishes of "loves" and "hugs" and "kisses." They were light on substance and questions, while heavy on weather reports and travel plans. They kept our communications anodyne.

As my condition worsened, my patience grew thin. Not to rain on her Rose Bowl Parade, but I felt she needed to know that things looked bad for me.

"Hello, Mom?"

"Hi, son."

"You got a minute?"

" . . . "

"Does that mean, no?"

"We're packing for California, but I've got a minute. Is everything okay? You feeling better? I lit a candle for you at—"

"Now, see, when you ask questions like that I start thinking that you honestly care about my health. But I know better. Your shame is too deep, your denial is too strong, and your husband is too fucked up to allow you to

133

come to terms with what I'm going through."

"That's not true."

"What part of that is not true?"

"I don't know what you want me to do."

"You do whatever you want. I just called to say that things are not getting better. The Ganciclovir isn't working. I still can't swallow and the hole in my esophagus has gotten larger. My crackpot doctor's given up. The nuns asked if I wanted to talk to a priest about last rites. I could only laugh."

"What can I do?"

"Well, you could tell your husband. He may be a bigot, but he's not stupid. He's got to know something's up. You haven't had the courage to tell him I'm gay, and soon, you'll have to explain how I died. That'd be fun to watch."

"Don't say that."

"Bullshit. I'm speaking the truth."

"What do you want me to do?"

"Talk to him. What's he going to do? Leave you? Just fucking tell him."

"What good would that do?"

"Nothing for me. I thought it might help you out, knowing you have someone you can talk to about the situation that I, your youngest son, am going through. Do you keep things away from him out of love for him? It certainly has nothing to do with any love for me."

"That's not fair."

"How dare you tell me what's fair and what's not.

You don't get to do that anymore. Only a mother can do that—and you've made it clear that you wish to be my mother as much as that husband of yours wants to be my father. I'd love to know how you're going to explain away my dead body."

"Please, please, please. Can't we just wait for the Rose Bowl to be over?"

She started to weep. I hung up the phone.

There's a line in Larry Kramer's play, *The Normal Heart*, which Peter took me to see at the Public Theater when I was a freshman at NYU. Ben, the protagonist's straight brother, says, "People don't like to be frightened. When they get scared, they don't behave well. It's called denial." This explains part of what my mother was going through.

About an hour later, after my friend Robin and I shared a one-hitter in the bathroom, the phone rang. Robin grabbed the receiver.

"St. Vincent's AIDS Suite 712," he answered. "How may I direct your call?" His face dropped. "It's your father."

"My father's dead."

"Do you want me to say that?" He handed over the phone.

I heard the man's tears before I even put the receiver to my ear. I had never heard this man, who had caused me to shed more than a few tears in my lifetime, cry.

He explained that he'd come upon my mother in a ball at the bottom of the stairs, cordless phone dangling from her hand. He insisted she tell him everything.

"Am I that terrible that your mother couldn't even tell me what's been going on?" he asked.

I'd had enough of their reindeer games. "That's not a conversation I need to have."

"What can we do?"

I laughed. "Nothing now. My lot's been cast. I'm not expected to live much longer. If I'm around when you get back from Pasadena, maybe you can come visit. Until then, I need nothing from you guys."

He tried to ask questions, but it quickly deteriorated into a stammer-of-consciousness. He confessed to not knowing much about AIDS except "the occasional mention in the Wall Street Journal." He said he put a call in to his doctor to get some more information, to ask about CMV, to find out what they could do.

I felt like I was talking to an overeager five-year-old. "There's nothing you can do. OK? Now, I'm tired, so we'll talk later."

"Yes, yes. Get some rest." I could hear my mom sniffling in the background. "Your mother says she loves you."

"Thanks. Safe travels." I hung up the phone and turned to Robin. "Let's grab a cigarette."

On New Year's Eve, around 11 pm, long past visiting hours, I was propped up in my bed watching a tiny Dick Clark freeze his ass off in Times Square. I felt more at peace than I ever had. It was nice to have the pressure of New Year's Eve gone. I had no interest in partying and no expectations to see much of 1996.

As a sign of how hopeless my recovery was, the nurses moved me into a private room that had opened up a few days before. This was an end-stage move. The nurses shifted us around like pieces in a Chinese puzzle and placed the doomed into the most dignified rooms available. Mine had southern exposure and was situated across from the nurses' station in the Spellman Building. In the hallway, outside my door, a plaque commemorated "the generous support of the Robert Mapplethorpe Foundation."

"Heeeeyyyyy, girrrrrrrrl!"

Joey's voice, as usual, preceded her. Her squeal echoed down the halls before she bounced through the door and shut it behind her. Chanel Number 5 filled the room. I had not seen her in years, and I certainly did not expect her visit.

As Joey would describe herself, she was "a character from way back," an army brat who ran away from her parents into the sinewy arms of New York at the age of 14. She quickly learned the tricks of the hustling trade under the guidance of a former priest who ran a homeless shelter just south of Penn Station. At the age of 16, she was hanging out at Max's Kansas City and Club 82, where she met the legendary International Chrysis, who became her mentor and eased her into the netherworld of gender fluidity.

In the '80s she met a benefactor who provided estrogen shots and plastic surgery. When she scoffed at

137

altering what she called her "money maker" to become a full, anatomical woman, the relationship ended. I met Joey through a few of the boy bar beauties, and although she never performed onstage, she dressed to be remembered in skintight mid-century Hollywood sexpot gowns plucked from her walk-in closet.

Joey always had an admirer or two on-hand to help her keep up the cavernous loft on 14th Street that she filled with 19th Century reproductions of furniture used in the court of Marie Antoinette, vintage lifelike mannequins, and taxidermied birds of prey.

She was in top form, her blonde hair was tousled like Marilyn in *Bus Stop*. Underneath her monkey fur coat, a bright purple macramé dress stretched across her figure like a fishnet glove.

"Joey! What—?! How did you get in here? Aren't you freezing? You look amazing!"

"I snuck the Widow in!" She displayed the bottle of Veuve Clicquot as if she were Carol Merrill. "I hope you have some cups around here."

She threw off the monkey fur and set her things down, then leaned in to kiss each of my cheeks. "Mwah! Mwah!" She made certain that her breasts, what she liked to call her "show udders," brushed against my face as she pulled away. "Happy Nineteen-ninety-… six? Is it six? Are there cups in here, girl?"

I pointed to the window ledge.

"Styrofoam?!! I can't drink from Styrofoam. The squeak makes my teeth hurt!"

"How did you get in here?" I asked again.

"Girl, I'm like a mist. I slip under doors." She unwrapped the orange foil on the bottle, untwisted the metal cage, and popped the cork. "To you, girl." She took a swig. "You look skinny!" She shot a jealous look. "Here."

"I can't swallow."

"Can't—or won't! There's more in it for you if you do." She laughed and took another swig. "Just put a little on your tongue. You can spit it out." She gestured for me to open my mouth. The champagne was bubbly and dry and puckered my tongue. Saliva pushed the remnants down my throat. I felt the burn in my chest and winced.

Joey took a swig from the bottle. She wiped her mouth with the back of her hand. "Nothing but class."

She then regaled me with stories of recent travels and distant conquests until a nurse popped her head into the room. She pretended not to notice Joey, or the bottle in her hand, or the areolae of her nipples popping through the expanding holes in her dress. "Happy New Year," she said.

"Happy New Year," Joey and I answered in unison. The nurse closed the door.

Joey examined a fake watch on her wrist. "What time is it? I need to be somewhere by one."

Dick Clark, back from commercial, announced the two-minute countdown to the midnight.

"Should we count down?" she asked.

"No. But thanks."

She toasted the crucifix above the door. "Thank Jesus!" She took another swig, then turned back to me and lowered her voice to a whisper. "That Jesus is H-O-T positive."

She began another round of stories, of broken champagne flutes wielded by spurned queens in Parisian lobbies and absurd invented dances perpetrated on unsuspecting clubgoers in Mexico City.

She went into the bathroom to check the mirror and let out a scream. "The light is HORRIBLE in here!! I don't know how you live with it."

She slipped back into her jacket and smoothed down its slick black hairs. "Great to see ya', hon." She kissed my forehead, then checked her imaginary watch again and turned to leave. As the door closed, I saw her look both ways down the darkened hall before darting off. The clickety-clack of her vintage heels faded away.

The following evening, I laughed heartily when I saw on the news that the USC Trojans beat the Northwestern Wildcats, 41 to 32, in the 82nd Annual Rose Bowl.

WAGSTAFF'S GHOST
(1988)

"I have only loved three things in my life: Robert, my mother and art."
—Sam Wagstaff to Patti Smith

"Right before you die, museums appear and want to know where
your money's going. Anyone who's sick gets it. It's really kind of ... horrible.
One museum called and asked me to donate a photograph in Sam's memory.
Before he was dead."
—Robert Mapplethorpe to Dominick Dunne

The only thing Robert hated more than St. Vincent's
was being *in* St. Vincent's. Especially in early July, prime
cruising season. He would have sworn he was in the same
room where Sam spent that dreaded Christmas of 1986:
same outdated bed, same tubes and machines, same view
of the Twin Towers, same metal crucifix with the

hunky Jesus above the door. 1986 was also the year of Robert's diagnosis, the year chills, swollen glands, and diarrhea became part of his daily existence.

"Put your mind somewhere else," said Patti, his best friend and wisest advisor, as close to a wife a gay man could get.

When she reached to take off his wool socks, he flinched and folded into a ball. Robert couldn't bare to have his feet rubbed. He knew she had done it for Sam, and Sam had loved it. But Robert didn't. Robert already had Patti's unconditional love. Just sitting together, reading Baudelaire and the *Times* out loud, gossiping about the art world, singing her beautiful lullabies. Robert needed nothing more.

Well, he might need an escape plan. Dr. Salzman had yet to assure Robert he would be released for his opening night. If they said he could not leave, Robert planned to disguise himself and catch a cab uptown to the Whitney. Come Hell or HIV, he would be there. He wished Sam could be there too.

He wondered how Sam could function in this place. How he could curate a silver show for the New York Historical Society while continuing to collect unique pieces for himself. It took Robert too much psychic energy to remain sane in the hospital. The thought of receiving dealers bearing Colonial-era serving spoons and mint-condition Deco tea sets was unbearable.

"Sam, think it over. Are you sure you know what you're buying?" Robert would ask.

Sam would only roll his eyes and continue to write checks.

We all deal in different ways, thought Robert. Sam dealt by trading the millions he made selling his photo collection to the Getty for glittering, reflective objects worth nothing more than their random places in history. Robert dealt with the loss of Sam by pushing his photography even further.

"Let's grab a smoke," he said, exhausted by thinking of Sam.

Patti sighed and shook her head. "Robert, they just took you off oxygen. You'll end up on a coughing jag and they'll have to call in that phlebotomist you can't stand to readjust all those tubes." She gestured toward his long, sinewy arm. He had always been thin. Now, his limbs were mere twigs. "Plus, you'll only run into that guy who's got a crush on you. He's probably waiting outside in the hallway right now."

"Don't you dare open that door!"

"I think it's romantic." Patti laughed heartily. Robert joined her hesitantly.

A young blonde lady in red and pink scrubs entered. "Glad to see you're up and laughing!" She looked about, expecting a visitor. "What's so funny? Your tv ain't even on." She grabbed his wrist and looked at her watch.

Robert looked around the room; Patti wasn't there. She was in Detroit. He'd spoken to her by phone last night. Sam had done the same thing at the end, talking to people who weren't there.

"How are you today, Nurse?"

"Oh!" She giggled. "I'm just a candy striper."

She took his bedpan to the bathroom, dumped it into the toilet and flushed.

"Candy striper" made Robert think of muscle cars and doo-wop. Did Patti's phantom visit cause a slip in the time continuum? "They still have candy stripers?"

"I guess." The question confused her. "Nurse Erika told me to come check on you." She made a frowny face. "They're awfully busy up here."

Robert held her with his penetrating blue eyes. "You've got great cheek bones."

She rubbed her reddening face with the palm of her hand. "Gee, thanks."

The door swung open. Dr. Salzman entered, pen clicking nervously. The candy striper seemed to shrink away and walk backwards out the door as if the tiny, pink-bespectacled man in the white coat was the Queen of England.

"Hi, Dr. Salzman."

"Hello, Robert. How are you feeling this evening?"

Sad, lonely, frightened, haunted by Sam, hallucinating visits from Patti. "I'm good," he replied.

"Well, I have good news. If you keep up this strength, it looks like we'll be able to get you out of here for your … vernissage."

Vernissage, thought Robert. Doc's angling for admission.

"Of course, with your latest strength tests, you might

have to attend in a chair."

"Carried aloft by Nubians?"

Dr. Salzman smiled weakly. "Wheels, I'm afraid."

"You free Wednesday night, Doc? Can I put your name on the list?"

Dr. Salzman played it cool. "Oh. Could you? That would be fun. Thank you, Robert. Plus one?"

"I'll tell my assistant when he makes his hourly deathwatch call."

July 18th was overcast, but the heat and humidity made Robert's skin come alive. No more sealed windows and canned, cooled air. He wished it could be summertime, but as his grandmother used to say, "If wishes were fishes we'd all be swimming in riches." If she could see me now, he mused. A couple of hired nurses wheeled him to the curb and helped him in to the back of a limousine. He knew there'd be no more trips to Fire Island.

The nuns and priests of Robert's Floral Park childhood told Robert all about Heaven. Robert preferred to think about Hell. Until Sam died. If Sam was in Heaven, would it be something like Oakleyville on a picture-perfect Wednesday afternoon in the middle of July?

As the driver made his way to Robert's apartment, they passed the Chelsea Hotel. Robert gazed at the great red façade and its zigzag mask of wrought iron stairs. Or maybe that's Heaven, he thought, an enormous building full of artists and sexy boys who read books. That's where

Sam would be. In a colossal room with Liberace on piano, looking over contact sheets with Peter Hujar, discussing philosophy with Michel Foucault, digging up Hollywood scandal with Rock Hudson. That's what Heaven is, that's where I want to be.

For the opening night of his retrospective at the Whitney Museum of American Art, Robert arrived in a wheelchair and allowed various acquaintances to take turns pushing him through the galleries. His hair whisked back like Dracula and he wore a black dinner jacket and black velvet slippers with monogrammed initials in gold thread.

Every picture made Robert think of Sam's initial reactions to them. Without Sam, there'd be no pictures on the walls. Without Sam, there'd be no Robert Mapplethorpe. Without Sam, Robert would know nothing about beauty, art, and inspiration.

Robert left the party fashionably early, just as Warhol taught him. He arose from his wheelchair in the entryway, assisted only by a black lacquer cane with a silver skull handle. Guests murmured as they watched his spectral figure glide across the Whitney's concrete bridge and vanish into the back an idling limousine.

END STAGE

"If I could have
Two things in one:
The peace of the grave,
And the light of the sun ..."

—Edna St. Vincent Millay,
Moritorus

Smoking, sun damage, tooth decay, politics, blocked calls, money troubles, talk of a cure: these are just some of the things you no longer care about when your doctor has given up on you and you're one of a chorus of guys awaiting your big death number on the 7th floor of St. Vincent's.

Oddly, I was at peace with the situation. I had no bills, obligations, or responsibilities. Neither my landlord nor my creditors could do anything to me as I lay dying. Dilaudid dulled my pain, visitors occupied my time, I had no need to concern myself with plans, expectations, or judgments.

I had one only resolution for 1996: to die quietly in my sleep—and not, if I could help it, on a malfunctioning hospital bed. I didn't have a stash of Seconals stored away above the fridge as Bobby had. But then my brain wasn't shrinking. I could still speak, laugh with my friends, read a book, wipe my own ass. Even though the end was near, how or when I would go remained a mystery.

I never envisioned my own death. Could I simply waste away? Would the ulceration in my esophagus grow and spread to other parts of my gastrointestinal system? Would the CMV spread to my eyes and cause me to go blind? How much longer could I survive on intravenous milkshakes?

Raucous ACT-UP meetings gathered at the Center, a repurposed red brick schoolhouse on West 13th Street next to the Overbite Building, around the corner from St. Vincent's. In weekly shouting matches, A-list fags and their lesbian admirers organized zaps and protests and mass demonstrations in Albany and DC to protest for expanded access to experimental drugs and better healthcare. We didn't discuss such nonsense on the 7th floor and channeled our anger elsewhere. We didn't hold much stock in salvation either. Especially from a government that viewed us as criminals and a medical-industrial complex that saw no profit in dying queens.

Timmy visited every few days, usually during his lunch hour from cutting hair. As the executor of Bobby's will, he tried his best to keep debt collectors and grousing family at bay. Foolishly, I thought being so near death excused me from all the drama, but on the second day of January, the floodgates opened when Timmy returned from Puerto Rico. He had a fresh tan on his sunken face and a mischievous grin.

"Just back from Heaven. Ocean Walk Guesthouse, in Ocean Park," he said, standing in the doorway, shaking snow from his coat. "Gentlemen only. Clothing optional. Spent the day between the pool and the beach. Dined by a bonfire in bare feet. Rum nightcaps with local boys."

"Sounds very Tennessee Williams," I told him. "Good thing you weren't eaten by the natives."

He sat beside my bed and handed me a box wrapped in blue and silver paper. "A belated Christmas gift," he said. It turned out to be a brown leather toiletry bag from a fancy shop on Madison Avenue. He acted as if he'd spent a lot of thought (and money) on its purchase. There wasn't much use for beauty products on death row, but I thanked him because my mother taught me properly.

I hadn't noticed Timmy's two-week absence, but feigned interest in his newfound enthusiasm for Caribbean sex tourism.

"We took a break from San Juan to visit El Yunque one day," he said. "It's the rainforest on the outskirts. It's like being in Hawaii, without the long flight." He railed against the "exorbitant price" to board Joe in a kennel the two weeks he was away. "You'd think they'd have special prices for such small dogs," he huffed.

We didn't mention of the anniversary of Bobby's death. I asked how the handling of his estate was

149

coming along.

"Fine, fine, fine" he said, in a manner that meant it clearly wasn't. After a few awkward beats, his snake-pit voice dropped to a whisper. "Look. Between you and me, and that hot Jesus hanging above the doorframe there, I'm getting a lot of grief from Bobby's family. His mother and his sister—never happy women to begin with—are very, very upset with me. And you. Even the brother's wife is trying to get him to change the tune."

"The tune?"

"That it wasn't suicide. They're trying to say that we killed Bobby."

With all the lying and living-it-up that Bobby perpetrated in his brief half century, he left the world penniless. His estate consisted of some fancy watches, some Tiffany baubles, a Brussels Griffon named Joe, and mounds of credit card debt. Sure, he had three life insurance policies, but those had been sold those off to viatical companies long ago. Bobby left no advance directives, and it certainly seemed suspicious that he changed his will two days before he died.

His mother, sister, and sister-in-law, over the half-assed objections of his brother, hired a lawyer to contest the will. In the meantime, they threatened to go to the police with accusations of murder. Even though they were fully aware that Bobby had chosen to end his life when he returned to New York, they believed Timmy (and I) had squirreled away his money. To my knowledge, there was no secret stash of cash, no massive fortune.

150

There certainly was no murder. Their threats were idle. They were trying to pressure poor extortable Timmy. There was nothing they could do to me.

"Relax," I told him. "If it'll make you feel better, I could film a confession that clears you of anything. Get a video camera. We'll make a video describing Bobby's last moments, from our flight back to New York to his bed to his death. I could say you weren't around at all. I don't care. What are they gonna' do to me?"

Timmy's dour face glowed. "Oh, would you? That'd be great. I'm sure I won't need it but … just for, you know, when you're—" He walked to the window. "It'll be a good thing to have. In case they play hardball. And who knows how long this nightmare will last?"

Playing hardball and nightmares are two other things you no longer care about when you're weak and tired and your doctor has taken off to Vietnam.

As the last existing gossip of Bobby's vanished circle, Timmy managed to slip in that Ken was "disgusted" with the way things went down. It sounded like a Ken word. I could hear him say it. "Dis-GUS-ted."

I couldn't blame him for his anger. He had always considered Bobby his best friend—and in many respects he was. But Bobby had done so much for so many, a lot of people thought he was their best friend. There were times I thought he was my best friend. Problem was, when it came to the end, Bobby was nobody's best friend. In life he was warm and wise and witty, open and optimistic. As he deteriorated, he grew angry and selfish,

151

closed off and off-putting, true only to himself. He knew his death was imminent, yet he chose to keep it a secret from his family and most of his remaining friends. Because of this, what he left behind grew into a cluster-fuck of soap operatic proportions.

Timmy explained to Ken that we did only what Bobby wanted. Bobby wanted Ken to be kept in the dark, just like his family. Ken was furious that he was never told about Bobby's "coward's way out." And he never liked Timmy, so Ken was doubly incensed to learn he'd been left out of the decision-making loop. Because of our toxic history, Ken held a special contempt for me.

A year before Bobby and I took off for Key West, Ken passed his second attempt at the New York Bar exam. By Christmas he found a job at what he called a "boutique real estate law firm," which meant he had a nice office but had to answer his own phone.

Nothing made Ken happier than his spacious one-bedroom on the 20th floor of 2 Fifth Avenue, with its sunken living room, smoking balcony, eat-in kitchen, and view of Washington Square Park. He got a thrill from being in the same building as Bella Abzug and longed to catch a glimpse of the ongoing feud between Larry Kramer and Ed Koch in the white marble lobby.

It was only a ten-minute walk from 2 Fifth Avenue to St. Vincent's, but Ken made a point of not visiting me.

I asked Timmy about Joe.

"The usual, adorable. Expensive, but adorable." He looked at his watch and stood. He encased his thin neck in the folds of a long rainbow scarf. "Must get back to work. Snip, snip!" He paused at the door before turning the knob. "When you're up for it, I'll bring a video camera in."

After Timmy left I fell asleep. A knock at the door woke me. A tall woman in a white lab coat and a stern Margaret Thatcher face stood halfway in the hallway and halfway in my room. Her rigid smile looked like a laugh fighting to get out. Her flowing auburn hair made her look half her age. Her green eyes were fixed on my chart as she greeted me with a cheery, heavily accented, "Happy New Year! I hope I didn't wake you."

She laid her long blue-white fingers over her nametag to hide her intimidating four-syllable surname. She offered her other hand in greeting. "Magdalena! Call me Dr. Magda. I'll be filling in for Dr. Ross while he's ... away." Her grip was firm, her skin silken.

"Dr. Ross is in Vietnam," I said, although I'm sure she knew. "He gave up on me," I added with self-pity.

Her lips parted and her face erupted into what seemed to be a silent chuckle. It took me by surprise. "You have had quite a few endoscopies," she announced. She laid my chart down and flickered her fingers before me. "Do you mind?"

"Be my guest."

Her touch was warm against my throat. "Nothing there."

She cupped my armpits. "Your lymph nodes are not particularly swollen." She examined my Port-a-cath.

"Very clean. Very nice." She consulted my chart again. "This protocol doesn't seem to be doing any good. The Ganciclovir hasn't closed the ulceration one iota. Yet, there are no further ulcerations. Nor are there any of the symptoms typically associated with CMV. I would like to try something different. Do you mind?"

"Try whatever you like."

"I would like to stop the Ganciclovir. I think cytomegalovirus may be the wrong perpetrator. And I have yet to see any sign of fungal infection."

Dr. Magda suggested I begin a regimen of a drug called prednisone. She suggested it might close the hole in my esophagus. Her exact words were, "It's worth a shot." She produced a shrink-wrapped package of 20-milligram peach tablets the size of watch batteries from her pocket.

"You'll take 40 milligrams, two tablets, each day for a week. Depending on how you do, we will then taper you off. We shall see how these work first." My water pitcher was empty. Dr. Magda went to the sink and filled it up. She was spritely despite her Teutonic facade. Was she new to the floor? So full of hope, she made my heart ache.

She popped two pills from the package and offered them like mints, then handed me a Styrofoam cup of water. Her beeper went off as I forced them down. "You may begin to feel much stronger than you really are," she warned, as if guiding me through an acid trip. "Systemic cortocosteroids can be deceptively powerful. Be mindful of your body. Follow my directions during the course of

154

administration. Yes?"

"Don't worry about that. I don't do much. Reading in bed, hallway walks, hanging with visitors, that's about all I can manage these days."

She grabbed at my hand in an awkward gesture of kindness. Then, just as suddenly, she gave me a business-like "I shall check on you tomorrow," and left.

The next morning, as the crew serenaded the floor, I felt constricted by my bed, trapped in a miserable room with sickening scents from dim hallways. What the fuck was I doing on the godamnned 7th floor?!

When Dr. Magda arrived, I begged her to let me out of the hospital for a few minutes to get some fresh air. I pleaded with her, so desperate I felt nearly psychotic.

"Oh, that'll happen," she said, her smile twitching. "Just breathe through it. How are you feeling besides that?"

"Better, I guess."

She handed me two more pills.

On the third day of prednisone, Kathleen came by with laced butter cookies from a clandestine cannabis club in the East Village run by an old guy who made them for chemotherapy patients. She then produced a plastic bag of store-bought hummus and pita bread. The smell of the lemon, the garlic, and the tahini made my mouth water. I dipped a finger into the chickpea paste and brought it to my mouth. I swished it around. It stuck a bit in my throat. With a sip of water, it went down without effort. I took another finger full. It went down smoothly.

The pain that I had known since the previous October was gone.

"It would seem that your dysphagia, concurrent pain, and extreme weight loss were caused by an aphthous, or idiopathic, ulcer," Dr. Magda announced on the fifth day of prednisone. "Both ulcerations can look very much alike in an endoscopy. Aphthous ulcers are obviously not as severe as cytomegalovirus. Picture them as glorified canker sores. It's an autoimmune condition, nothing to do with immuno-deficiency. Anyone can get them."

I sat up in bed with a ravaged half-gallon of chocolate chocolate chip ice cream before me. A glorified canker sore? After all this shit. Part of a family that subsisted on neglect and judgment, my childhood was an obstacle course of stress-related health problems. My mouth filled with raw pink spots on a regular basis. My lips budded with cold sores that left scabs that lingered for weeks and scars that remain to this day.

In the third and fourth grades, a few years after my mother divorced my father, married his best friend, and enlarged the number of older siblings I had by five, I had facial shingles and stomach ulcers in quick succession. As a kid I was a walking autoimmune disorder, bound together by frayed nerves and strengthened by the knowledge that I would escape to New York one day.

By the time I had finished the initial week of prednisone, Dr. Magda had the milkshake removed from my arm. With the help of Kathleen's pot cookies and the occasional bathroom joint, I managed to retain a few pounds. I knew things were on their way to getting better when Dr. Magda told me they would take the catheter out of my chest and release me from the hospital.

After months of carrying the Port-a-cath around, after my own cells had grafted themselves onto its tube as if it would be part of me for the rest of my life, the procedure to remove it the following morning was anticlimactic. It was quick and painless, but I can't say I felt free.

Winded, weak, and frail, I made it home in an old Checker cab that reeked of Aramis, the cologne my father wore. Although it was frigid outside, the days were getting perceptibly longer.

I took a long, hot, catheter-free bath, flipping through old *National Geographic*s until my fingers pruned like the pages. I stood naked in Bobby's bathroom mirror. I knew from my last examination that I weighed a measly 125 pounds. In a well-lit, full-length mirror, I could see what that meant on my 5-foot 9-inch frame. I'd always found myself too thin and small in a *Pumping Iron* society. After more than a decade of benches, curls, dips, squats, and laps, I was sallow, concave, and emaciated at the age of 28.

My mother called and said she and my stepfather wanted to visit. (It was out of the question that I would visit them.) Whether they meant to seek forgiveness or assuage their guilt, no matter, I was in no mood for a pilgrimage. It seemed my survival was due to heartfelt prayers, votive candles, and a Catholic hospital named after the most reliable of saints. In her mind, my being alive had more to do with the spiritual minions of St. Vincent.

I wanted to prove her wrong. I wanted to unveil her blind faith and disrupt her system of denying away the unpleasant. Part of me wished I would have died to teach her and the rest of my family some sort of lesson, but my survival instincts were too strong, my will to succumb to a spiteful death too weak. I told her I needed some time. I needed to gain some weight, increase my strength. I was eating again and retaining pounds, but I couldn't go to the gym yet, and certainly couldn't run. I did as many pushups as I could each day. I needed to reinhabit my previous shell. I figured Easter might be a good target for my mother and her husband to shoot for.

At the end of January, Adriana moved back to her childhood home upstate, near Saratoga Springs. Her father had grown ill, and she wanted to go up and play the piano for him. Contrary to the upbringing most of us had, Adriana's childhood was Rockwell boring. She had loads of friends in high school, accepting parents, functional siblings, piano recitals. While a surprising number of downtown queens challenged and belittled Adriana's transition, her family thought nothing of it. Barry, Chiclet, Adriana. She had always been the same person to them. Now she was just bigger, prettier, more fun.

One evening before she left, Adriana invited her friend, Cedar Gottlieb, to visit the penthouse. People were still greeting each other with "Happy New Year," but we were well into 1996. The February issue of *Vanity Fair*, which hung on the magazine rack by the toilet in our bathroom, featured Cedar and her work. "Diane Arbus for the Fin de Siècle," they dubbed her, whose photographs "threw down a gantlet at the teetering feet of the culture wars." The writer applauded her portrayal of "marginalized comrades, the 'other' so often seen only in art house documentaries or in the back of a squad car."

Cedar, the magazine gushed, was "the high arbiter of drug-and-drag-chic." Whatever that was. Cedar owed her intimate circle of fame to Adriana and Joey and Connie and JoJo and Cody and Kathleen and all the others who permitted her to detail their nightly exploits with the 35mm camera she carried everywhere she went.

She came to the 7th floor with Adriana once, her camera around her neck, on her way to a biennial in Oslo. She acted as if she was visiting the apartment of a barely tolerated aunt. "It never changes . . . " She shivered for emphasis and looked around almost wistfully. "I've been here more times than I care to count."

She took a few pictures of me in my hospital bed. She never displayed them. That is, I didn't make the cut. By 1995 she had a surfeit of snapshots documenting the plague, renowned images of dying friends, ones with the courtesy to follow through.

She asked about my pending eviction; it was apparently common knowledge. I told her that the people who owned the penthouse, disappointed that I did not die, were gunning for me again. The $9,999 Bobby gave me to retain his lawyer had run thin, and since Bobby had refused to sign a renewal lease a couple years back, there was no official lease for anyone to live there. They were tolerating Bobby until he died and did not anticipate my arrival. To them, I was merely a squatter with AIDS.

"That's so very '80s," Cedar replied.

She wanted to help me out, said she didn't want me to end up on the street like so many of her friends. "Talented friends," she added, as if their artistic abilities made their loss more insulting.

"Let me give you a print," she said. "When you need to sell it, let me know, and I'll get you some cash for it."

My favorite picture of hers, "Chiclet waiting for profiteroles, Madrid," was the one I thought of first, but I wasn't going to ask for it. Cedar's work sold for thousands of dollars.

"Chiclet waiting for profiteroles, Madrid," hung in the Louvre. It was a Fotofolio postcard. Although none of that mattered to me. It's a great picture in which Adriana—or rather, her earlier drag persona—loiters before a carniceria on Calle Cervantes. A ravaged Fiorucci denim jacket barely contains her breasts, so her cavernous décolletage is on display. Like her heavy day-drag eyelids, her lips are greasy and parted slightly. She is conscious of the camera but feigns unaware, twisting her profile away coyly. Her summer-kissed skin echoes the tones of the cured pig legs that dangle in the windows behind her.

"Maybe we could make a trade?" Cedar asked, and by

the time she left that night, we swapped my final 60-count bottle of 10-mg hydrocodone tablets for an original dye destruction print of "Chiclet waiting for profiteroles, Madrid" measuring 25 ⅞" high by 38 ½" wide. But not, she cautioned, one of the "official" edition of 25 prints that had been sold out through the Prater Flume Gallery since they were first shown in 1993. Cedar would make me a pirate print that would remain unsigned until I needed money. "But let's keep that between ourselves. Just remember, when you need to sell it, come to me. Don't go to Prater Flume or an auction house."

Even though homelessness loomed ever closer, I had no interest in the cash value of the counterfeit print, and I didn't care if it was signed. "I don't want to sell it," I told her. I loved that picture for sentimental reasons. "Don't forget who was out getting the profiteroles."

A week later, the picture arrived via messenger in a black vinyl tube. I took it to the framer even though I knew my days in the penthouse were numbered. I also had a suspicious feeling I wasn't quite clear of the 7ᵗʰ floor. My appetite remained, but I never regained strength. With the prednisone (and painkillers) out of my system, I grew exhausted easily and began to take frequent naps.

By Valentine's Day I had lost touch with nearly all of the people who had visited me on the 7ᵗʰ floor. Compared to St. Vincent's, Bobby's penthouse felt like a mausoleum. I ignored the periodic ringing of the phone and buzzing from the intercom and wallowed in the misery of my hobbled freedom. Some friends chose to avoid me once I'd cheated death. Others, as friends do, simply drifted away. The majority had wagered on mourning me. My recovery robbed them of another tragedy in their Rolodex of suffering. It's hard to keep up sympathy for someone you've already buried in your mind.

Peter called one day, out of the blue. He told me he was relocating to LA, but keeping the lease on his apartment near Lincoln Center. He seemed surprised, almost disappointed, that I was out of the hospital and free of the Port-a-cath. "You can throw the first shovel of dirt on my coffin, how's that?" I asked.

Kevin started dating a guy, a back-up dancer for Madonna. He spent his nights at the guy's apartment out in Brooklyn. The maid's room became his daytime office and craft space.

One night, while he was away, I let myself in. I tossed a pile of his t-shirts to the floor and sat on Bobby's Aeron chair. It seemed like years since I'd slept in that room, since I'd met with Bobby and Timmy about spending the winter in Key West, since the day we returned and the morning we said goodbye and I slept for 36 hours and woke up with a scratch in my throat. It had only been a little over a year.

Kevin was mid-audit, his bed piled with seven years of receipts and invoices for the various entertainment ventures he ran like a low-budget David Geffen. On Bobby's old desk lay his latest enterprise: the stuffed blue swordfish that once hung above the bed. Half of its body was covered with silver and blue Swarovski crystals that Kevin had taken to gluing on individually.

Back on the stifling 7th floor, on threadbare polyester sheets and rubberized mattress pads, waking up in a cold sweat was not uncommon. After a month out of the joint, I started to drench Bobby's Frette sheets at the night. A deep, dry cough consumed me, producing nothing but a frothy spit that coated my tongue. I took to sleeping long stretches of the day. Once I managed to drag my ass out of bed, it felt as if my chest were in the grip of a vice. My morning pushups dwindled briskly, from 18 to 12 to 7 until I gave them up completely. To get sustenance, something easy, like chocolate milk and egg salad sandwiches, I'd bundle myself like a bag lady and step out to the deli. People three times my age passed me left and right on the sidewalk, a few with walkers moved faster than I could shuffle. After a distance of a few blocks, I was soaking wet and winded.

Dr. Magda brought me in for x-rays. The pictures showed scarring on my lungs: the left was full of what looked to be storm-gray swirls, the right was halfway there. With a note of admiration, she told me I had the worse case of PCP she'd seen since doctors began to prescribe Bactrim (a horse pill containing trimethoprim and sulfamethoxazole) for those whose T-cells were below 200 and in greater danger of contracting PCP. Dr. Ross took me off Bactrim prophylaxis months ago because I couldn't swallow the pills. He didn't prescribe aerosolized Pentamidine in its place because I doubt he

163

thought I'd make it through CMV to fall prey to PCP. I never got the chance because I never saw Dr. Ross again.

As I waited into the evening for a room to open up, I watched two maintenance men in blue overalls slap pink, red, and lavender hearts along the walls. When the men came to the doorway, they unfurled a banner made from pastel cardboard conversation heart decorations and took turns on a shoddy stepladder to raise them high: "LET'S KISS," "CUTE STUFF," "SOUL MATE." Meant to be cheery, they were a rude reminder that healthy people were fucking each other for Valentine's Day.

Because I needed the best oxygen set-up they had outside of ICU, I ended up in the Coleman section of the 7th floor, in a private room that faced the direction of the sunset. Across Seventh Avenue, on the scalene triangle where 12th Street and Greenwich Avenue bisect, stood the hospital's utility building, a windowless red brick jumble of right angles, metal doors, and rolling gates emblazoned with graffiti. It buzzed throughout the night and into the early morning with deliveries of food, linens, medical equipment, cleaning supplies, oxygen tanks, while waste the hospital couldn't incinerate was carted away.

That first evening back, long after visiting hours, I lingered by the window, hooked up to my oxygen tank and intravenous Pentamidine. My fever had mounted and my temples throbbed like the valve on a pressure cooker. Plastic tubes blew a steady stream of oxygen into my nostrils. Although the hallway was unusually quiet and infomercials had taken over all seven television stations, the situation was not conducive to sleep.

Around 4:30 or 5:00 in the morning, as the sky lightened to blue, I saw a pair of men in black leather stagger across Greenwich Avenue. Obviously drunk or otherwise high, they held onto one another for support. They paused in a fit of laughter to lean against the black metal railing that surrounded the triangle. Soon, they were kissing. Their big bodies tangled. Their heavy breathing appeared as white clouds in the February air. I was a bit delirious at the time, my temperature hovered around 100 degrees, yet I knew they were a couple of apparitions on their way home from the West Side bars, a sexy gay mirage, the kinked-out spirits of Sam Wagstaff and Robert Mapplethorpe, masculine frames wrapped in the shiny dyed hides of dead cattle, a fantasy ripped from the sketchbooks of Tom of Finland's notebooks. Their appearance was for my entertainment. I coveted their drunken, sloppy joy. Perhaps one day, I might experience such passion again. But that meant living. And living meant hope.

The next day, my cough grew worse. I could barely blow the red ball up the translucent tube they'd bring me every morning to test my lung capacity. By dinner I thought I was a goner: my body shook, my vision was clouded, and my fever spiked to 104 degrees. It was one of those code blue nights on the 7th floor with screaming and scrambling up and down the hallways. To the nurses, I was a hangnail during an explosion.

Unsure what fresh Hell my latest installment on the 7th floor might bring, I kept my stay under wraps. But that night, as my brain baked and I resolved myself again to die on the 7th floor alone, a trio of friends appeared unexpectedly in my doorway: Annie, Lucy, and Mike, who had been fellow workers from my time at Restaurant Florent. They'd been around the corner playing with material for a new show at P.S. 122, a riff on James Whale's 1931 *Frankenstein,* when the impulse to visit me struck.

They had not seen me since their rehearsals began and were surprised to find I'd been moved to another room. Eventually, they deduced that I'd been released from the hospital for the CMV a few weeks back and had been readmitted for PCP only now.

In my delirium I thought Annie and Lucy and Mike were there to perform, that we were all backstage in a dressing room. I could tell by their faces I was in bad shape. It was clear that the floor nurses were overwhelmed and unable to answer my calls, so like the well-rehearsed team they were, they gathered around me: one at my feet, one at my torso, one at my feet. They applied cold washcloths to my forehead, neck, and chest. They held my hands and massaged the inside of my wrists and elbows. They ran out to get me orange Gatorade. They told bad jokes and laughed as if we were out drinking. Far into the night and long after visiting hours, they remained until my fever broke.

At some point in the shivering haze, my father

appeared. He wasn't the broken, smiling man I knew. He was younger, as he looked in the curled-up, sepia-toned photos from his time in the Navy. I doubt his apparition was legitimately supernatural, yet his presence felt more substantial than a hallucination. He never spoke. He gave no explanation for his visit, asked no forgiveness for his slow suicide from a slew of bottles, and offered no promise of closure. He simply lingered for a bit at the foot of my bed and smiled. His blue eyes twinkled. Then, as if distracted by an attractive nurse, he wandered off.

My father was sensitive and funny with a penchant for getting sloppy drunk. Deep down, he was an artist forced into the role of a corporate cog in much the same way his wife, my mother, was a closet broadcaster trapped in the dual roles of high school teacher and suburban housewife.

The official cause of my father's death was sepsis— brought about by decades of drinking and smoking, advanced Crohn's disease, and poor diet. His heart died many years prior to his physical end. After my mother left him and married his best friend, his life consisted of enduring alone, keeping his spirits up, and drinking through his pain. At the end, most of his organs shut down and he died hooked up to a battery of machines, unable to eat or breathe on his own. His passing was reminiscent of so many on the 7th floor.

Once my temperature dropped to 99 degrees, I felt a sense of relief that morphed into guilt. I thanked Annie,

Lucy, and Mike but they overrode me with wagging fingers and shaking heads. "No, no, no, you'd do the same for either of us." Which was true.

The three began their usual chitchat as if nothing had happened, the kind of snarky gossip I liked at my bedside, smart conversation without my participation. They began to discuss upcoming travel plans, which led to scheduling conflicts, and then, somehow, technical cues on their new show, until Annie and Lucy began their inevitable argument. Mike rolled his eyes. I mustered a belly laugh through my agony and exhaustion.

Annie and Lucy had studied dance in college and worked together ever since. Rumor was they were lovers, which only increased their downtown cachet and the size of their audience. Only one of them identified as an on-and-off lesbian. Yet they were such an old married couple—and Mike was their stage son, musical director, and backstage referee. Once their argument reached a pitch equal to my fever, Mike dutifully shuffled them out of the room and out into the New York night for cocktails.

At the end of February, once the "Erin Go Bragh" shamrocks and shillelagh-wielding leprechauns began to fill the hallways, I was declared well enough to be released.

When got back to the apartment, the final set of eviction papers were taped to my front door. My retainer had long been used up. Besides, I was tired of fighting. Now that my health was clear, homelessness loomed, but

I suspected I might get better quicker without the constant aggravation to keep what wasn't really my home. I spent the month of March avoiding everyone and everything.

Adriana was upstate and Kevin moved to Brooklyn. I told him to take the washer and dryer and for anyone else to grab whatever fixtures they might want. The landlords would get their place back, just stripped of everything Bobby and Stewart and I had put into it.

The phone rang less and less. Peter left two messages, one from Basel, Switzerland, and another, a week later, from his new home in Beverly Hills. I hesitated calling him back out of my shame. We'd both arrived in New York ten years prior to chase our dreams. He was living his in grand fashion. I was barely alive and dead broke. I hesitated to ask him if I could stay at his place on the Upper West Side. It was sitting empty, and I was without a home.

I hated the obvious pleasure he got by saying, "Yes, please stay at my place until you get back on your feet."

Timmy showed up unannounced one day as I was packing my books away. He was eager to see when I might record that confession regarding Bobby's death. I feigned weakness and fake-coughed a lot just to get rid of him. I told him once I was completely free of the PCP I would gladly commit my confession to Memorex.

When I told him I expected to be evicted by June, he wondered aloud how much money the landlords might get from the next tenant. He looked about the living room wearily. "That is, after they put some work into it."

I was still recovering from my second brush with pneumonia, just off my daily regimen of aerosolized Pentamidine and another round of prednisone. I had many more pounds to gain. Yet I felt better enough to see my mother and her husband, so they arranged to visit me at the beginning of April, the weekend before Easter.

When I was a kid, the two of them took business trips to New York fairly often, staying in a corporate suite at the Essex House on Central Park South. They stopped visiting once I lived in the city. The last time they'd been to the city was in September, 1985, when they dropped me off, bright-eyed and bushy-haired, at the Judson Hall dormitory. My mother cried as they pulled away in the family station wagon. That was the last time the three of us had been together in the city.

Even though Adriana and Kevin were gone and the penthouse was nearly empty, my parents took a room at the crumbling Gramercy Park Hotel, a short walk from East 10th Street. Their room on the third floor was painted an industrial green. The duvet cover and matching pillowcases were vintage: once shiny gold, now a pilled beige. Only one of the bedside lamps worked, which was fine because my stepfather wasn't one to read. They had a view of the park, gated and locked below, with its empty winding walkway, bare trees, and brown patches of earth from the record-breaking winter.

My stepfather grabbed the tv remote and found a golf game on one of the wavy channels. "No cable," he huffed to no one in particular as he propped himself up on the sagging bed to settle in for a visit he clearly wasn't thrilled about. I was still alive, but he certainly wasn't excited to see me. I suppose I preferred his detachment over his tears.

Despite our seemingly revelatory phone call, he was as ornery and antagonistic as ever. Perhaps he thought it best to act as if nothing was wrong, dirty water under a shaky bridge. In that spirit he treated me as he always had. He goaded me with off-handed wisecracks and remarks about the Clintons.

He continued to tease my mother in front of me, which drove me doubly nuts. He remained in their hotel room to watch tv while my mom and I took short tours of safe spaces like the Macy's Orchid Show, the Folk Art Museum, and the Rose Reading Room at the New York Public Library.

My mother acted attentive and doting, somewhat overdoing it, classic case of too much, too late. I felt like a flimsy shell and didn't want to be hugged.

During the course of their stay, there were no great eruptions or revelations. We avoided the upcoming presidential election, and although they sheepishly inquired about my health, we never mentioned AIDS. No one stormed away or raised their voice. I managed to stay medicated enough to get through the weekend without conflict.

Things were raw between the three of us—but they had been for years. A shrink once described our dynamic as an Oedipal triangle. I successfully argued that I was stuck in the plot of *Hamlet*: a mercurial boy out to vanquish the man who killed his father and married his mother. Of course, murder here is metaphorical. Alcoholism, Crohn's disease, a broken heart, loneliness, many things conspired to kill my father. And my mother was no Gertrude. Locked in an unhappy marriage, saddled with three kids, unable to pursue her dreams in life, she fell in love with another man and found herself with the enhanced brood she was woefully unprepared to rear.

I suppose I expected a *Terms of Endearment* moment, a circling of the wagons, feelings of acceptance and forgiveness all around. Instead, we play-acted roles of caring and appreciative family and trudged through their 84-hour visit.

Once they'd left for the airport, I noticed I no longer held that *Hamlet* rage. They lived their lives the best way two people in their situation could: haunted by shame and buoyed by their love for each other. My father may have been a victim of their betrayal, but his problems ran deeper than that. His death was suicide, not murder.

I surrendered the penthouse to the landlord at the end of May. Peter let me crash on his couch while he was in LA. When he returned to the city, he helped me find a studio on Greenwich Street, two blocks from the Hudson River.

As rainbow flags sprang up across the Village, a letter from my mother arrived. Alongside her heartfelt note of thoughts and prayers, still remarking at "what a wonderful lark" they had when they visited in April, was a clipping from the *Wall Street Journal*. Dated June 14, 1996, the front-page center column and its continuation on page A6 were stapled together and folded to fit into the legal envelope.

"New Drug 'Cocktails' Mark Exciting Turn In the War on AIDS," read the headline. "Companies Race to Market With 'Protease Inhibitors' After Good Test Results." After 20 months on the multidrug treatment a 39-year-old former dancer is quoted saying, "I'm excited. I feel strong. I feel hopeful. I feel normal again."

I was terrified. "Excited, strong, hopeful." I understood those words as concepts, I didn't feel them. And what exactly was "normal again"? I had just found a new home and had no idea how to pay the rent. I had just overcome my third bout with PCP. I didn't want to think about AIDS anymore, much less undergo an intense daily schedule of pills that caused a load of symptoms and required constant refrigeration.

My old friend Andrea from NYU called. She was now living in D.C. with her husband and new baby. She said she'd read about the cocktail in *The Washington Post*'s Sunday supplement and asked if I'd be taking it.

I felt as if I'd barely survived the best that western medicine could do for me. Why would I give them another shot to take me out? Couldn't I just wait a few years until we knew for certain it wasn't AZT all over again, another poison by prescription?

"I see," she replied, shifting gears. "And how's that mushroom tea enema working out for you these days?"

"It was bitter melon, and I get your point, bitch."

VITO GOES TO THE MOVIES
(1990)

"I wish my life was a non-stop Hollywood movie show,
A fantasy world of celluloid villains and heroes,
Because celluloid heroes never feel any pain
And celluloid heroes never really die."

—Ray Davies,
Celluloid Heroes

"I'm young and I'm strong and nothing can touch me."

—Bette Davis,
Dark Victory

Even as a kid Vito worshipped the Silver Screen, the
studio system, its shining stars. After a long-fought war
newly won, the American mood was ripe for arrogant
beauty, unbridled lust, hell-bent vengeance, and people
who spontaneously broke out into song. For a gay boy at
the daily mercy of neighborhood toughs, a movie ticket
granted Vito an attainable retreat from the real world,

two hours alone in the dark with permission to desire.

The Church had already rejected Vito. When he was 10, he revealed to Father Zumpano, in the confessional at St. Paul's back in East Harlem, that he held passionate feelings for Tarzan. Or rather, the succession of half-naked men who played Tarzan on-screen. He confessed that he preferred the blond Lex Barker to the darker Gordon Scott. Not that he wanted to be Jane—unless we're talking Jane Russell, he giggled nervously, she's really got the best part: all the delights of the jungle with none of the work. And that body? The kind of guys you could land with that body? Am I right, Father?

He asked if his interest in the bodies of comic book jungle men (he didn't dare bring up *real* men like Tab Hunter and Rock Hudson) meant he would be damned to eternal hellfire. Yes, Father Zumpano sternly confirmed. You have queer leanings, and if you do not fight them, you will be rejected by society and unsuitable for entry into Heaven.

This didn't seem right to Vito. He saw plenty of men like himself in the movies. Usually bit players, flouncy and effeminate, the butt of jokes and recipients of gratuitous violence, but their existence, larger than life before an audience of witnesses, confirmed that Vito wasn't alone. On July 11, 1964, the day Vito turned 18, he made his great escape from the Hell that was Lodi, New Jersey to Greenwich Village, to recreate himself and find his own Lex Barker.

The island of Manhattan stoked Vito's passions and

made him come alive. Twenty-six years later, he still felt as if he was starring in a series of movies. Even here, on the 7th floor of St. Vincent's.

Vito rebuffed his mother's entreaties to come home so she could nurse him in his childhood bed. "I'd rather die in New York than live in New Jersey, Ma," he would tell her. The irony of lying here, dying here, in a Catholic hospital, was not lost on Vito. Neither was the sunset view out his window.

Seven stories down, across Seventh Avenue, on a piece of land shaped like a pizza slice and surrounded with black wrought-iron fencing, an amorphous assemblage of squat brick structures operated as the loading dock and disposal site for the hospital. From above it looked to Vito like the set of a German expressionist film.

Kids skateboarded along the triangle's slanted brick base. Neither they nor their yuppie parents would ever value the history of their new neighborhood. Vito knew they'd never take notice of the plaque on the Greenwich Avenue side of the hospital's incinerator commemorating the resuscitation of the uncle of Village poet Edna St. Vincent Millay, and in turn, the genesis for the poet's middle name. They would certainly not appreciate the faded tablet noting that Georges Clemenceau, the prime minister who led France through WWI, once lived here. Bronze plaques, Vito knew, were transitory, as useless as human memory.

There was nothing to mark the triangle as the location

of the hallowed Loew's Sheridan. On a childhood field trip to the Newark Museum, Vito spotted what would become one of his favorite paintings, "The Sheridan Theater," a dreamlike Edward Hopper canvas from 1937 featuring a Bette Davis-type from behind in the back of a stipple-darkened mezzanine.

On June 15, 1957, when Vito was only seven, Billie Holiday packed the Sheridan in a rare New York appearance. Long before the curtain rose, mobs of people lined the triangular sidewalk to see Lady Day. Twenty-five hundred people got in, more than 500 were turned away.

Obsessed with the old movie palaces, Vito located *Times* microfiche from the September 18, 1921 opening of the Sheridan. The *Times* reporter called it "the newest and most pretentious motion picture house." The premiere bill consisted of singers George Dale and Dorothy Bell, a short movie called *Here and There in Greenwich Village*, and the main attraction, *Disraeli*—the silent one, not the 1929 remake that netted an Academy Award for George Arliss (who starred in both films).

The show palace served as a footnote in the Lindbergh baby kidnapping. In 1933, a sharp-eyed cashier notified the authorities about a customer who purchased a 40-cent ticket with a marked bill from the $50,000 ransom. Vito loved the irony of this small moment in history because the kidnapper, German carpenter Richard Hauptman, never got to see the end of James Whale's *The Invisible Man.*

By the time Vito got to the Village, the Sheridan was a

dilapidated eyesore. The late '60s wasn't a time for jazz concerts and movie palaces. In the summer of Stonewall, the New York archdiocese snapped up the property to build housing for the staff of St. Vincent's. During the theater's demolition that September, a portion of brick wall from the structure collapsed, killed a passer-by, and sent another across the avenue to the ER.

The following year, Vito marched with the newly formed Gay Activist Alliance from Christopher Street to Seventh Avenue across Greenwich Avenue. They paused between the old Sheridan and the hospital.

"DIEGO WAS PUSHED!" they shouted. "IT'S TIME TO PUSH BACK!"

Armed with placards and pamphlets and insults directed at the police, the young demonstrators blocked southbound traffic for hours. As night fell they switched to candles. It was one of the first in what would be a life full of protests. Switch up the outfits and beef up the boys and you had yourself an early ACT-UP demonstration.

Vito gave a speech to ACT-UP in 1988 that would become his boilerplate pep talk. "Someday, the AIDS Crisis will be over," he would shout to whoops and hollers. "And when that day comes—when that day has come and gone, there'll be people left alive on this earth—gay people and straight people, men and women, black and white, who will hear the story that once there was a terrible disease in this country and all over the world, and that a brave group of people stood up and fought, and in some cases, gave their lives so that other people might live and be free."

The crowd, who'd already started clapping at "a brave group of people," always went wild when Vito emphasized that final phrase, "might live and be free." To die peacefully and be free seems the best he can now hope for.

He wished he could see a movie. A new release. With popcorn and people around. Not a VHS tape on a giant tv rolled into his room on a demonic metal cart. And nothing fancy like the Ziegfeld or the Paris. Vito just wanted to go downstairs to the Art Greenwich Twin at the far angle of the hospital's scalene loading dock. Named for its side-by-side screens that showed high-brow movies, the Art Greenwich Twin was a hastily assembled duplex with cramped seating. It was no Loew's Sheridan.

From his window, Vito could see the marquee of the Art Greenwich Twin. *Postcards from the Edge* and *Goodfellas* were playing. In his wobbly state (half of what he once weighed, anemic, unable to keep food down), he would prefer the company of Carrie Fisher's words and the camp pairing of Meryl Streep and Shirley Maclaine over Martin Scorsese and the violent hijinks of Joe Pesci and Robert DeNiro.

The last movie he'd seen was *Ghost*, back in July. He was still furious that Whoopi Goldberg's character turned back into Patrick Swayze before kissing Demi Moore at the end. If the love between the young potter and her yuppie husband had been true love, argued Vito, the climactic kiss would have been just as beautiful and meaningful, if not more so, with Demi and Whoopi locking lips. But no, Hollywood had to switch out the black woman for the white man at the last minute so as not to alienate the audience.

Vito posed the idea of slipping away to see *Postcards from the Edge* to his frequent visitors, Adam and Tony, a young couple who met cute at an ACT-UP die-in outside the Center for Drug Evaluation and Research in D.C. Adam was blond and Tony was brunette. Other than that, everyone thought they were twins. Vito called them his angels.

Tony arranged flowers. Adam sat in the cracked Eamesian chair at the foot of Vito's bed.

"You think the doctor would give you an AMA?" Tony asked.

"Christ, more acronyms."

"You think he'll agree to a leave against medical advice. You'll have to pack up and get out. Once the movie ends, you can't just be readmitted. You'll have to wait down in the ER all over again."

Vito knew St. Vincent's was strict that way. Patients who left the building without clearance were considered dismissals. Their beds would be changed promptly, their flowers, cards, and personal items tossed into bags and sent to the incinerator.

"Besides," added Tony. "You can barely make it to the bathroom on your own."

181

Vito pouted. He looked as he must have when he was 10. An emaciated 10-year-old with a moustache and a bald head, but 10 nonetheless. "I want to go to the movies."

"Well, you can't, Blanche!" The twins answered in unison. Vito stuck out his tongue. Good thing they were cute.

On their walk home that evening, Adam and Tony passed the Pink Pussycat on Bleecker Street. Slings, handcuffs, lubricants, floggers, and blow-up dolls in a variety of poses cluttered the front window. Adam stopped. He grabbed Tony's arm. Hmmm, they thought. Vito was no bigger than a blow-up doll.

The next day the couple presented Vito with an O-mouthed inflatable, a blonde bob wig, Jackie O. sunglasses, and a trench coat. They explained their idea. Vito agreed that it sounded like a bad movie, but his trickster's smile revealed he was willing to give it a try.

They decided on the 2:35 showing, which took place during the height of visiting hours and the lull of the midday nursing shift. Vito slipped into his street clothes. Adam walked him to the elevator, down to the lobby, and out the revolving door on 12th Street. Tony remained with "Vita," as they'd named the doll filling in for Vito, tucked into his bed with the covers up. If a nurse popped in, Tony would run interference and claim that Vito wanted to be left alone to sleep. The movie's running time was 1 hour 41 minutes, with roughly 10 minutes of trailers. They had a little over two hours to pull it off.

Vito skipped the popcorn and the Raisinets. Just the smell of the concessions was enough to revive his spirits. The theater was only a quarter full, and Vito's favorite spot remained, left aisle, halfway from the screen. Adam helped Vito into his seat. He kept his coat wrapped around him. As the lights went down, he rose out of his sick body and hovered like smoke particles in the projector's beam. AIDS no longer existed. Just sight and sound and a flickering screen. Vito's body tossed about like a kid at the circus as he laughed. Adam had never seen him so alive.

UNDETECTABLE

"History, Stephen said, is a nightmare from which I am trying to awake."
—James Joyce,
Ulysses

"Joyce is right about history being a nightmare—
but it may be the nightmare from which no one can awaken.
People are trapped in history and history is trapped in them."
—James Baldwin,
Stranger in the Village

What began as a tickle in my throat in the summer of 1995 devolved into a tough time swallowing by October. Until I was diagnosed correctly, pain and starvation caused me to ricochet in and out of St. Vincent's well into 1996.

I was too busy fasting with pariahs and entertaining fools on the 7th floor to care about the real world snippets that played out on passing television screens: Christopher Reeve paralyzed! Unabomber Manifesto published! Government shutdown! Whitewater! Blizzard of '96! O.J. Still Not Guilty!

Trapped in a tenuous present, I surrendered any interest in my future. To rise above the physical and psychological pain, I played the past over like a VHS in my mind. I fought despair through nostalgia. I pictured the nightclubs, warehouses, and basements my friends and I frequented.

I laughed at the memory of throwing wadded-up dollar bills at HRH Princess Diandra as she channeled Patti LaBelle on a stage the size of a four-seat tabletop. I missed drinking and smoking and laughing, dancing all night to mammoth speakers with shirtless men and glittering queens, seeking out anonymous sex, divvying up hits of cocaine in crowded stalls, walking home through charged streets, a life that was far behind me, replaced by a non-stop kabuki fueled by Dilaudid and sugar water, accompanied by a chorus line of haggard souls on their last legs, my own danse macabre.

When I was released from the hospital in January of '96, Kathleen brought me a green book with blank pages and encouraged me to write again. I carried it around with me but wasn't ready to fill it with words until Wednesday, October 23rd, when I wrote in confident, Catholic-school script:

"After long hours of thought, full of self-disgust, bitter over the declining state of my health, I've decided to begin anti-retroviral treatment. It seems to be working for people. I hate to think of it as some sort of last-ditch effort, or surrender to Big Pharma, but that's just what it is. I suppose it makes sense that the drugs inhibit the protease enzyme that HIV needs to reproduce, but, like AZT, I'm leery of Rx companies pushing pills like cornflakes. And I will question the HIV=AIDS theory until I die. Yet I've signed on to be a hapless volunteer stuck to a daily regimen of pills. 18 pills down my gullet each and every day now until I die is overwhelming. But then I think, Bobby would have killed for this opportunity."

My foggy journey into "HAART"—the strained acronym for "highly active antiretroviral therapy," more sexily known as the "cocktail"—began the previous Monday during an appointment with Dr. Magda. I needed another round of antibiotics for a wicked case of "folliculitis," a mellifluous name for a rash of nasty mini-boils that appeared along my ass and down the back of my thighs. The good doctor noted my other symptoms: malaise bordering on fatigue, low-grade fever, shallow breathing. I was also coughing, but then I had been running a few days a week while struggling to give up cigarettes, again.

I wasn't as worried as she seemed to be.

"We should be careful," she warned. "The PCP could return. Any number of things could spring up."

I surrendered peacefully. "Fine," I said. "Write the scripts. I'll take the cocktail. What do I have to lose?"

Dr. Magda was unable to hide her delight as she scribbled out three prescriptions and a "pre-maintenance" schedule for me to follow: a protease inhibitor called Crixivan (indinavir sulfate) in the form of a big yellow capsule taken three times a day, joined by two nucleoside analog reverse-transcriptase inhibitors (or NRTIs), a red and orange capsule called stavudine (d4t) and a bone-white diamond-shaped tablet called lamivudine (3TC), both taken twice a day. Like the prednisone, this was just the starting dose. The amount of daily pills would gradually climb to 18 a day.

To alert me to each dose, I set an alarm to go off every eight hours: nine o'clock in the morning, five in the evening, and one in the morning. Each drug had to be taken on an empty stomach; I couldn't eat less than two hours before, or one hour after. Regardless of the contents of my stomach, taking the meds made me feel nauseated much of the day. Cannabis gave me an appetite. Without the evening munchies, I would have never gained back my fighting weight.

Insomnia colored my nights, already day bright thanks to the amber streetlights that streamed in through my bare front windows facing Greenwich Street. I no longer looked out the sliding glass doors of Bobby's and on to the Grace Church steeple as I had on East 10th Street. Gone too were the sunset views from the 7th floor.

Now, I slept in a twin bed tucked into a cubbyhole, sandwiched between a shallow closet and a stall shower. Instead of a headboard, I had a window that opened onto a dim airshaft populated by a flock of pigeons, whose constant cooing and wing flapping I tried to drown out with CDs on constant rotation. Whatever I did, my mind fought sleep. And sleeping pills were out of the question because my alarm would snap me awake at one in the morning for my third dose of Crixivan. I feared drifting into beta sleep because shocking nightmares, like bad acid trips, would bolt me awake.

By Thursday, before I was supposed to up the dosage to the full 18 pills, things worsened. Around noon I was completely incapacitated, unable to stand for more than 10 to 15 seconds at a time. I was nauseated and dizzy, sick to my stomach like nothing I ever experienced as a frazzled little faggot with grown man stomach ulcers. I called Dr. Magda. I thought maybe I overdosed.

"Oh, that will happen for about two weeks," she said calmly. "But you cannot stop taking them. I know that it is unpleasant for you now, but if you stop them you could do serious damage." Previously, she had discussed counter indications and possible side effects. I had no idea how severe they would be. As time went on, I was unable to distinguish side effects of the drugs from symptoms of illness. Sometimes I just wanted to curl up and vanish.

Each morning I woke up depressed, confused, uncertain. Around 10, an hour after ingesting my morning dose of three pills, diarrhea would strike. I learned to have cooked white rice on standby. Around noon, my body would be consumed with what felt like flu. Throughout the afternoon, my gums and tongue would go numb and a metallic taste would permeate the soft tissues of my mouth as if I'd been snorting cocaine.

After my first structured week as an AIDS guinea pig, I rallied myself to keep from giving up. "I can live through this," I wrote, in a steadier hand than the day before. "I can be happy. I can enjoy what little bit of youth I have left." Deep down, I knew none of this was certain. The only guarantee I had was the inevitability of more side effects.

It had been about four months since my mother mailed me the clipping from *The Wall Street Journal*'s front page touting "New Drug 'Cocktails.'" I called her to let her know that I had finally given in. My will to live, it turns out, was stronger than my need for her to be wrong.

She said she was "overwhelmed" with my decision to take the pills. She had been afraid to follow up after she sent the article, she didn't want to seem to be pushing anything on me, it needed to be my decision. She wondered why I'd been so resistant. After all, bottles of pills kept her husband functioning. Modern medicine kept him alive despite his failing body and deepest wishes. Then my mother told me she was proud, which I found curious. Adriana said it too, when we spoke on the phone. Robin and Anna sent congratulations from Spain. Everyone was happy for me, but I was miserable.

"I can't fathom getting used to this or my body 'adjusting' to this barrage of stomach-churning chemicals," I wrote on Sunday, October 27.

"It's been hellish. Splitting headaches are the newest side effect. My brain feels shrunken and loose; when I move my head, it feels like it's sloshing around inside my skull. The GI stuff remains. My appetite hasn't quite returned, so I force-feed myself some fruit and granola so I can take my pills without too much discomfort. I throw a Pepcid into the mix to try and eliminate the gassy

189

feeling that always follows. The first four hours after a dosage is the worst—dull constriction of the lower GI tract, "coke mouth," body weakness and muscle aches (wherever any muscle tissue remains), a speedy, disoriented feeling, and now these headaches. Feel one coming on now."

If Bobby had lived, I wondered, how would he react to the cocktail and its side effects.

"Quality, not quantity," was his mantra. By which he meant, the quality of his life counted for more than the quantity of days he could eek out of it by taking toxic substances that made him wish he were dead.

On Thursday, October 31, 1996, a year to the day I entered St. Vincent's with misdiagnosed cytomegalovirus, I wrote, "I hope these motherfuckers work."

I noticed progress at the end of November when I began to tolerate the medications better. By my first post-cocktail blood draw in December, the levels of HIV in my blood had dropped and my T-cells had climbed. The following blood draw, in March of 1997, my "viral load" (the amount of HIV in my bloodstream) was under 200 copies per milliliter. Dr. Magda called it, "undetectable."

When I found out I was positive in 1990, my T-cell count was 2. Seven years later, they were above 500. Slowly but surely, the side effects began to calm down and my energy rose. I ate properly, ran regularly, and joined the New York Sports Club on 14th Street, which wasn't scene-y like the new breed of health clubs sprouting up but had enough fit fags to keep me motivated.

People no longer saw me as having AIDS or being infected with HIV. Sometimes, I'd even forget about it myself. But there was always something there to remind me: handfuls of pills three times a day, harried trips to the toilet, this sexy Israeli guy with premature salt-and-pepper hair and the body of an underwear model. I'd seen the guy around at the gym, and one day, he came up and introduced himself. By that point, I'd put a little meat back on my bones. I felt a little more like my old self. I passed for healthy.

The Israeli and I exchanged names. I did my best to tamp down any trace of desperate enthusiasm in my voice, as well as the hard-on developing in my sweatpants. He smiled warmly, leaned forward, and put his lips beside my ear: "Are you clean?"

I was confused. Now? Here? In the middle of my workout? Was he OCD?

"I shower pretty regularly," I answered.

He shook his head. His voice dropped to a whisper, "Are you positive?"

So this would be my new closet? In a society quick to condemn, being healthy-looking and undetectable gave me another reason to hide. When I passed as a straight man, it was an instinctual mode of survival. Passing as HIV-negative could be seen as criminal.

"You know what?" I snapped back, to my own surprise. "I refuse to answer that. It's offensive and appalling."

He rolled his eyes. "It's the way it is. I'm just trying to be safe, dude."

"You could try condoms, *dude*."

"Condoms, *right*," he laughed as he headed off to join the line for the elliptical machines.

I used to think that coming out stories were like assholes: every queen had one and cultivated it proudly. But coming out isn't a single event. Doors have hinges. By nature they open and close. Coming out, I realized, is a graduating continuum of self-acceptance, bravery, and opportunity. The process never ends.

The first time I came out was to myself, freshman year. This was the easiest because I'd long suspected I was gay. To celebrate the occasion completely, I drove down to Chicago to cruise up and down Halsted and Clark, the streets north of Wrigley Field that I learned as a kid were mad with faggots. I was still too shy to score and drove back to the suburbs, deflated.

The second time, the first time I came out to another person, was the result of a lame suicide attempt my senior year of high school, before I finally got laid in the city. My friend Susan was a wise ex-hippie with three adorable kids and a loveless marriage. She was also a student of my mother's when she was in high school.

We met at a local school called Greasepaint and Spotlights where we took improvisation classes with a bunch of local high school and community college kids. We clicked the moment we met. I enjoyed being in the company of smart, older people, and she enjoyed the same from younger men. More than a few people, my mother included, thought Susan was my "Mrs. Robinson." None of them knew the truth. Only Susan knew the truth. More so than I.

One afternoon, home from a miserable day of senior year, I rummaged though my mother's bathroom drawer and found a box of Sominex with 8 pills left inside. I swallowed them, slowly, dramatically, then reclined on my bed and dozed off. I was still alive when Susan honked the horn of her green Nova just outside my bedroom window. She honked again. In my stupor it took some time to process that Susan was in the driveway to pick me up for our improv class.

When I emerged from my home, she thought I was high. Once we hit the road, I told her what had happened.

"I'm bisexual," I finally confessed after she asked me what it was that would make me want to take my life. As a virgin, I thought bisexuality, even heterosexuality, might be a possibility for me down the road. Plus, "I'm bisexual" seemed to carry less shame than "I'm gay."

Susan pulled her Nova into a passing drive-thru lane. She put the car into park and turned to me. "What do you mean, 'bisexual'? Do you like women?"

Of course I liked women. What kind of a monster did she think I was?

"Have you slept with a woman? Or a man?"

I shook my head, no, as she put her car into drive. We inched a bit further.

"Would you like to sleep with a woman? Or a man?"

"I guess I'd prefer to try it with a man. I don't think about women that way."

The car approached the microphone. "What do you want to eat?"

"Just a Coke. It'll keep me awake."

"You need to eat something, you idiot. You just took 12 sleeping pills."

I ordered a cheeseburger and a Coke. As my eyes revived, I dropped my head and cried on her shoulder. "Just be thankful they were over-the-counter and not the serious shit." She rubbed my hair at a distance like the proper mother she was.

We never discussed it again. I never felt the need to bring it up, until I met my first boyfriend, Dale, on North Clark Street, the summer before I left for NYU. Susan continued to be the same friend I'd always counted on and admired.

The third time I came out, I was drunk and desperate and tried yet again to diffuse the situation by using, "bisexual."

I was a junior. Roman was a graduating senior. We wandered into the woods from a graduation kegger, passing a bottle of Jim Beam between us. Flashes of moonlight through the swaying trees overhead caught Roman's shining eyes and glistening lips. He suggested a game, a sort of Truth or Dare truncated to an outright Dare to Tell the Truth. "I'll tell you something no one knows, then you tell me something no one knows" were the basic rules. It seemed like an open invitation to me. I hoped Roman might share a similar truth. We passed the bottle back and forth in silence.

"My father beats me," Roman confessed finally. We did not have a similar truth, after all. "No one really knows. My sisters, of course. They go through it, too. And my mom. But she denies it. She just explains it away. 'He's trying to make you a man,' she says." Quoting his mother brought glowing tears to his cheeks.

"I can't wait to get to college, get away from him." He lowered his head and parted a handful of his silky brown hair to reveal a red slice along his scalp. "See this? Did that to me in the basement last week for fumbling the ball against Stevenson."

We finished the bottle. Roman wiped his eyes with the front of his t-shirt. His stomach was as flat and smooth as a river rock. My third coming out was not going to be easy, certainly not worthy of a letter to *Penthouse Forum*. I took the cue from Roman and stalled as long as I could.

"I'm bisexual," I mumbled.

Roman's face was still, his eyebrows raised, his nostrils flared, frozen in a combination of surprise and disgust. He had no follow-ups, didn't care to know more. When he spoke up again, he said he felt cold, and since the Jim Beam was empty, perhaps we should return to the party. We walked back in silence and parted with a half-assed hug.

The following Monday I was the class faggot. They

had me pegged. I wasn't bisexual. On the Kinsey scale (I had yet to discover), I was a complete and utter six.

Neither moving to New York nor being in the theater made coming out any easier. I came out to those I cared about, mostly girls who got the wrong impression and had to be informed to spare their feelings. I came out and came out and came out until my only circle of friends and associates were gay men and drag queens, at night, in clubs and bars, where we could dare to be ourselves without closets.

In the boy bar days, some of the queens, like Adriana, started to tuck regularly, beat their faces 24/7, and endure painful facial electrolysis because who wouldn't rather live day-to-day, undetectably, if given the option?

I came to New York eleven years ago to live an uncloseted life. Now I had to come out all over again. But I wasn't *just* HIV-positive, I was a full-on AIDS survivor.

The final entry in the green journal is dated February 2, 1997.

"Just got off the phone with Timmy," I wrote. "When his number came up on the Caller ID, I thought, if that queen thinks she's getting any videos out of me, she's sorely mistaken. But it wasn't about Bobby—not directly. Ken's dead. Brain tumor."

"Ken's … passed," is the way he said it. The melodramatic pause and the timbre of his voice could not hide the pleasure he was feeling. Timmy got a thrill out of outlasting his enemies. "I—I wanted to call you as soon as I found out … but I've been so busy helping his parents arrange the memorial at his apartment."

Ken never invited Timmy to his apartment at 2 Fifth Avenue, never wanted him to step foot in there, yet there he was, orchestrating an event with Ken's parents.

When I asked about the brain tumor, Timmy replied, "Funny thing, it was your grandmother's everyday cancer. No relation at all to AIDS. But who knows? Queens have been dying long since time in memoriam. Long before AIDS, or HIV, or whatever we're supposed to call it now. Just read *Dancer from the Dance.*"

I had just turned 19 when Ken brought me to Fire Island and Bobby gave me his first edition of *Dancer from the Dance.*

"It's an elegy as much as a chronicle of the madness," he said, parroting Bobby's pedantic monologue. "Sex, death, broken hearts, dead queens, mass drownings, overdoses, beautiful suicides, 12 guys burn to death in the Everard Baths." Like Bobby, Timmy considered AIDS just part of the continuum of gay victimhood, a long line of "*Camille* queens sprawled out on their daybeds, coughing away."

To resist my own urge to lounge about and look for blood in my handkerchief, I went back to work that summer. It was too easy in those days to live on disability. I needed to get on with life.

I followed some friends who were editing an "outdoor magazine" produced by Hachette Filipacchi's Custom Publishing Department so that Philip Morris could push cigarettes to what they referred to internally as "yams" and "yafs" (young adult males and young adult females).

In 1998, the major tobacco companies and the U.S. government reached the Master Settlement Agreement. In the hushed tones of the Philip Morris point-people with whom I dealt from day to day, it was called "the MSA." A large part of the MSA forbade tobacco advertising in magazines that catered to teenagers. So Philip Morris came to Hachette to create *Unlimited*, an oversized, full-color "adventure" quarterly, complete with alpine vistas, off-road racing pictorials, and rodeo features, all in the service of pushing Marlboro Reds. I'd come back from Hell to land a job with Satan.

It was hard returning to an office, but the schedule was flexible, hourly freelance work with good pay and fairly simple duties. I helped edit *Unlimited*'s state-by-state events section. I'd call around the country to local city halls and Elks' Clubs and gather information about seasonal events to reprint in the back pages. Charity golf events, chili cook-offs, 5-K runs, and their ilk would then be compiled into calendars and embellished with tongue-in-cheek headlines and pun-padded copy.

A typical entry might have read something like this:

WHEN IRISH THIGHS ARE MILING
It doesn't matter if you leprechaun or lepercan't at the 8th Annual Middletown St. Patrick's Day Weekend/Robert "BaBa" O'Reilly 5K Run to benefit the Middletown Police Department and St. Patrick's Food Pantry. At the finish line, forsake the pot of gold for an afternoon of fun: amusement rides, gun safety demonstrations, free CO_2 alarms, and face painting—if you're into that sort of thing. *Middletown City Hall, 7:30 pancake b'fast, 8:30 5K Run; "BaBa" O'Reilly FunFest takes place all day.*

We created pages and pages of this kind of tripe four times a year, for two months on and one month off. Editing a quarterly publication with Big Tobacco was lucrative work. So were the custom publications we were printing for other blue chip companies like Sony, Cisco Systems, Cadillac, and Mercedes-Benz.

At home I began to receive messages on my machine from a man with a thick Queens accent. I could never catch his name. "Sargent Wahwahwah," he'd mumble, "I'm a peace officer. And I need to speak with you." I replayed the tape several times to make sure he hadn't mumbled "police officer," but he clearly said "peace officer." I didn't know what the Hell that was and thought to myself, just don't call him back. It's not like he's the police.

In bed at night, with my head just feet from a shaft overrun with cooing pigeons, I thought maybe I was being investigated for my previous disability claims now that I had gone back to work. Perhaps it was someone working for my old landlord, trying to wrench money out of me for past rent. Maybe it was Chase Manhattan Visa coming for the debt I ran up thinking I'd be dead before anyone came to collect. Maybe it was Bobby's family causing trouble.

One morning, as I rushed through the lobby to get the elevator up to my office, I noticed two men speaking with the doorman. They wore similar dark suits that magnified their physical differences. One was small, round, and bald, with black hair over his lip; the other was taller and thin, with a stooped posture and long, gesticulating arms.

A fire hydrant with a moustache and a broken coat rack, I thought, just after I realized they were cops. I pretended not to see them and continued to the elevator bank. The doorman pointed me out of the crowd. They approached me, called my name, and flashed their badges. The fireplug announced in the Queens accent I'd come to know from my answering machine, "We're peace officers and we'd like to talk to you."

I wasn't playing dumb when I asked, "What does that mean?"

"We're here to investigate a possible murder," answered the coat rack. "We can do it here, or we can do it in our car, quietly."

The doorman sneered as the officers led me away. As we walked down the marble corridor to the revolving doors on 34th Street, I explained that I would have called the fireplug back and spared us all the *Law and Order* scene if he had just said on his phone messages that he was investigating Bobby's death.

"We're not allowed to give more information than necessary over the phone," answered the fireplug as we got to the black Town Car at the curb.

The coat rack opened the back door. I got in. The fireplug got into the driver's seat and the coat rack sat shotgun. The front doors slammed in unison. When they turned around, their faces were obscured by the headrests. Between their heads, in the rear view mirror,

I watched cars pull in and out of the McDonald's drive-thru at the intersection behind us.

Before they had a chance to ask a question, I said, "It wasn't murder."

"Yeah?" asked the fireplug. "Then tell us what it was."

The coat rack took out a pad and scribbled away as I rambled.

It was a series of expanding holes in his brain, the inability to read a book, hold a conversation, control his urination, wipe his own ass. He had lost the quality of life, his great loves, most of his friends. He didn't want to end up on the 7th floor or in a hospice somewhere with his mother saying rosaries at the foot of his bed. He wanted to live out the rest of his life on his own terms. It was his choice from the get-go and when it was time to go—and we always knew the time would come, even though I did everything I could to help him—we hitched a puddle jumper from Key West to Miami and a 747 to JFK. I carried him on my back through three airports to get him to New York and into his own bed in his own apartment, where he stupidly changed his will the day before we called the doctor to give him the shots before I fed him pink Lillys between bites of Cherry Garcia.

Tears streamed down my face. I told them how I slept as he died. How I felt his spirit leave his body, leave the apartment, leave the city, head into the atmosphere like a balloon. How I awoke to find Timmy and the doctor filling out paperwork. How I missed Bobby. How much he mean to me. How I should be dead, not him.

The officers nodded. My lungs heaved. I grunted uncontrollably. Snot ran down my lips.

The coat rack flipped his pad shut. The fireplug was already facing out the windshield. Someone said, "You can go."

I can go? Like a blubbering child, I used my shirtsleeve to dry my face. I looked at the backs of their thinning heads. "Is that it?"

One of them answered, "Yep. That's all we needed to hear. You shouldn't be hearing from us again."

The coat rack got out and opened the door for me. I stepped onto the sidewalk and decided to take a long walk around the block. I felt as if I'd stepped out of an abrupt confessional, without any Our Fathers or Hail Marys as penance. No sin I ever shared with Father Harry at St. Gilbert's caused me such emotion.

Of course, the peace officers had probably heard every variation of this story. During the plague, all sorts of people died in all sorts of ghastly ways while all sorts of family and all sorts of friends fought over what sorts of deaths they would share in the obituary. When I turned the corner onto 10th Avenue, the town car was heading east on 34th Street.

LAZARUS REDUX

"How wicked it would be, if we could, to call the dead back!"
—C.S. Lewis,
A Grief Observed

Lazarus couldn't sleep. The celebrations held in his honor had subsided, but he was still restless. Scribes from far and wide called upon him at all hours of the day and night. People beat drums and shouted his name when he passed in the street.

"There goes Lazarus, Revenant of Bethany!"

Women offered food, men offered their daughters. Every day brought a new feast in his honor. None of it gave Lazarus any peace.

He had been young once. He dedicated his life to serving the poor while most of his friends headed off to Jerusalem to study the inscription of Latin and network with the high priests.

One day, without warning, a shroud of inexplicable suffering descended upon him, a bludgeon of pain that took a toll on his body and left him bedridden, emaciated, speckled with strange lesions; he slipped in and out of consciousness, awaking periodically to beg for sweet relief.

His sisters, Mary and Martha, were desperate to spare him from so much suffering, so they sought out the help of an old friend, Jesus, whose mystical abilities were the talk of Galilee and Judea.

Jesus changed water into wine at a wedding in Cana, fed masses with a few fish and some loaves, healed lepers and the lame, gave the blind sight. Some said he even resurrected the dead. And he did it all without charging a single denarius. Certainly he can save Lazarus, the sisters thought. After all, we've known him since he was in the manger.

They sent a messenger to find Jesus and ask for help. When the messenger returned, he told the sisters that Jesus would be with them in a few days.

"A few days?!" Martha was incredulous. "We'll be sitting shiva by then."

"We simply have to trust him," Mary told her sister.

Lazarus took comfort in the fact that Jesus would not be showing up with his 12-man posse to work his hocus-pocus. Lazarus had been through too much already. He had lived a good life to endure a horrific illness. The way he saw it, he deserved to slip away with some dignity. He did not want to be "saved."

The following morning, Mary and Martha found their brother's body limp, lifeless, an empty vessel, his eyes open and a smile on his face. After the traditional three days, he was entombed.

On the following day, Jesus walked into town and told the despondent sisters to take him to their brother's tomb. The tears streaming down his cheekbones did nothing to reverse the fact that he'd arrived too late.

Martha scoffed and rolled her eyes.

But Mary had never seen Jesus cry. He usually acted like such a bad ass. "I appreciate it, Jesus. I really do. We both do—despite Martha's attitude. But he's gone. Lazarus is gone."

Martha leaned in. "He's been dead four days. If we roll away that stone, it will stink to high heaven."

"Trust me," Jesus replied, wiping his eyes. "Do you not believe in me?"

Mary and Martha wanted to, especially with all spectators that had gathered around them. But their brother was dead and gone.

"We sent you a messenger when he was sick," said Martha. "We were assured you would be here to save him. But—it's too late, Jesus."

Jesus smiled and opened his arms. "Roll away the stone and he shall be saved," he said. "All of us shall be saved."

Mary and Martha rolled their eyes as the crowd cheered. They unsealed the tomb.

Lazarus was beyond confused. He heard voices, but

was unable to decipher words. He no longer felt pain. Just a little discomfort. His back was cold and wet; his legs and arms, constrained. A soft breath brushed against his face, and a sliver of light cracked the obliterating darkness. Slowly, it expanded until the warm camel eyes and tyrannical smile of Jesus hovered just above his eyes. Mary and Martha stood beside him. Behind them, the citizenry of Bethany.

Lazarus tried to sit upright. Linen burial bandages restricted his movement. Once he realized he was on a cold slab of rock, he began to lose his balance. Jesus raised his hand and Lazarus steadied.

"Take off the grave clothes and let him go," Jesus said. The bandages slipped away.

Two nurses from the almshouse helped Lazarus to his feet as the crowd began to shout for Jesus.

"Noble Nazarene! My mother lost her legs in a mill accident!"

"Please, Jesus! You must help my son. He is possessed by demons!"

"Touch my belly, Miracle Man, so that I might bear a healthy child!"

Jesus raised his hands. "Good people, look. Jerusalem awaits." He assured the people begging for his assistance that he would return and help them in ways they could never imagine. "If you believe, I will do more than heal your earthly suffering. I will bring you eternal salvation!"

These were the last words Lazarus heard Jesus shout as he and his entourage headed off to the big city.

Before his resurrection, Lazarus of Bethany was just a regular Essene. Like his sisters, he helped out at the almshouse. He lived for his weekly trips into Jerusalem to study the Torah with his uncle. His family had no political ambitions. They weren't even on Rome's watch list.

All of this changed once word got around that the man considered public enemy number one by both the Pharisees and the Romans had resurrected Lazarus from the dead.

Let others worry about my safety, Lazarus thought. Secretly, he wished someone would whisk him off into the desert night. He could not recall feeling such despair. Martha was outraged when he told her he felt suicidal.

"But you've got color in your cheeks, Lazarus. You're gaining weight!"

Mary tried to be understanding. "Why not take a trip to the Red Sea? Fishing might be the just thing to take your mind off all of your anxieties."

But Lazarus was free of anxiety. If anything, he was angry. And who cared if he was gaining weight? All he wanted to do was sleep.

"You're selfish. That's what you are," said Martha.

"I'm selfish?" Lazarus spit the words. "I'm selfish. Your magic man uses me to prove that he's the son of God, to thumb his nose at the establishment. I heard he even cried. Well, I'm not just some unwitting pawn in the service of his ego. I was at peace with death. I made my farewells to the world. I never asked to be reawakened. I didn't sign on to be a magician's assistant. And you, dear, wise sister, never contemplated what it might be like for me to come back from the dead. This was never about me. I didn't ask for any of this. Who is the selfish one?"

Try as they might, their brother could not be moved, so Mary and Martha, as doting mothers and dutiful wives, left their brother to his own devices.

The day after Passover, word spread like locusts: Jesus had been taken from his bachelor Seder and brought before Governor Pontius Pilate. Some reported the Nazarene was up for execution. Lazarus suspected Roman propaganda, high priest gossip, and maybe even a few of Jesus's apostles were responsible for the rumors. Certainly this was another scheme for publicity. Pilate wasn't known to kill political prisoners—and even if he did, wouldn't Jesus revive himself with the sorcery he had used on Lazarus? Lazarus knew first-hand how powerful the magic man's media skills were.

It turns out Jesus's powers were no good to save himself. The man everyone relied on for salvation was helpless, deserted by God and the masses that once followed him like hungry dogs. On Saturday morning, Lazarus awoke to the news that the man who brought him back to life had expired on the cross. No wonder the weather had been shit.

A few weeks later, as rumors of Jesus's ghost roaming the desert spread like a haboob, Lazarus headed off for Jerusalem. Within days and without looking, he met a man from Damsacus named Ahumm.

Smart, attractive, and full of healthy skepticisms, Ahumm steered clear of politics and organized religion. He experimented with meditations from the Far East and forsake meat. In no time, Ahumm gave Lazarus a sense of peace he'd never felt before.

For the remainder of Lazarus's unexpected second life, the two provided each other with the patience of the cypress and the fortitude of the oak tree, growing older and wiser together, but never in each other's shadows.

ANOTHER LIFETIME

"I have learned to fail. And I have had my say."
—Edna St. Vincent Millay,
Lines Written in Re-capitulation

It's been 35 years since I heard AIDS mentioned in a fifteen-second report tucked into the middle of the evening news. I was a freshman in high school, just coming to terms with my desire for men, firmly convinced I was not going to change, priesthood or not. The only reason I paid attention at all was because news anchors didn't often say the word "homosexuals." And a disease that struck them exclusively seemed like something I should keep an eye on.

Twenty years have passed since my winter on the 7th floor at St. Vincent's, another lifetime. I no longer pass the asphalt asterisk formed by the improbable intersection of 7th Avenue, Greenwich Avenue, and West 11th Street on a daily basis. These days, I live uptown, at the northern end of Manhattan.

It was time to move. The West Village became an open-air mall, a celebrity chef food court for the rich and the aspiring. The neighborhood that once housed abbatoirs, artist lofts, nightclubs, sex clubs, and Restaurant Florent has been erased by haute hotels and high-end retailers. And tourists wait in line to wander the revamped Highline.

The piers I roamed as a troubled young fag have been redesigned as lush parkland with glass towers multiplying in size and number along the West Side Highway and the river towns of New Jersey constructing a mirror image skyline across the Hudson.

Where boys carried on in the bushes and queens did runway among the ruins, moneyed brahs lug golf clubs to Chelsea Piers and leery-eyed nannies push trust fund children in pricey strollers. Smiling first dates kayak and paddleboard where we once spotted bloated rats and human bodies with some frequency.

A couple of millionaires are building their own island park where survivors of the Titanic docked and gay men cruised their lives away.

Giant box stores are inevitable.

Over on Greenwich Avenue, Uncle Charlie's, where I first met Ken, is now a phony Irish pub called Fiddlestick's. They weathered the sign out front to make it look authentic, as if one of New York's most popular gay pick-up bars never existed there. At the sidewalk tables, hipster millennials down their drafts and stare at their iPhones, unaware of the bewildered spirits around them. They don't care about the history of the neighborhood. They certainly don't want to hear about the time that death hung in the air like bad patchouli. They just want to know how to get to the Highline.

St. Vincent's is a phantom, virtually undetectable in its new role as another Habitrail for the one-percent. Flying debris killed a woman walking down West 12th Street during construction, so the signs touting "The Greenwich Lane" were removed. Who knows what they're calling the place now?

I like to think of *Poltergeist*, the Tobe Hooper original from 1982, not the godawful 2015 remake. I envision the ghosts of St. Vincent's rising up one night, perhaps after the Village Halloween Parade has died down— or better yet, on December 1st—to wreak havoc on the latest gentry.

Noguchi coffee tables flip into the air. Nelson saucer lamps flicker wildly. Hästings bed frames creak through the night. And as fast as you can say, "JoBeth Williams," the residents will snatch their children and Uber away in horror.

Sure, they moved the bodies and the machines and some of the hospital's buildings, but they forgot to exorcise the souls of all those who suffered and died here!

A group calling itself the New York City AIDS Memorial, funded by a bunch of bold-faced names who wouldn't have been caught dead in St. Vincent's, commissioned an enormous mishmash of white beams at the far west angle of the park where the utility building and incinerator for the hospital once stood. Grids of triangles on angular panels form legs that meet at the concrete covering decades of toxic remnants of medical and radioactive waste. The memorial evokes an abstract albino spider—a sluggish hybrid of Sol LeWitt and Louise Bourgeois. How this memorializes the AIDS crisis is unclear.

The Overbite Building across the street now serves as the slick, new Lenox Hill "Healthplex." Remodeled extensively and renamed for a real estate investor and his wife, The Phyllis and William Mack Pavilion provides emergency ambulance service, a state-of-the-art imaging center, outpatient surgeries, physical therapy, and medical offices. It's a far cry from its days as a DMV for the sick and indigent, but its round, white teeth are still intact.

Some Christians like to talk about being born again, but my Lazarus situation was nothing like that. Receiving a new lease on life felt like a combination of hair-trigger terror and gun-shy hope. I never felt particularly lucky, or saved, or enlightened. I felt more like a bamboozled wraith, my face pushed into a pile of my own mortality. The pall lifted, but the nearness to death remained, like an antibody in the bloodstream or a wicked case of nostalgia.

I know it's sick to be sick about a time when I was sick, but St. Vincent's destruction haunts me. (*A Moveable Plague?*) The neighborhood's transformation and my banishment from it only heighten my yearning for a time when surviving was more important than living "*exactly* where you want to live."

I'm playing the long game now, nearing 50, an age I never imagined I'd reach. I'm smart enough to know that AIDS is not over by any means. It's merely lost its punch. But then, so has being gay. We're no longer criminals. We serve openly in the military. We won the right to marry. Western society has begun to embrace the fluidity of sexual identity and the flexibility of gender lines.

AIDS movies—part cheap sentiment, part call to action—are no longer guaranteed Oscar fodder. AIDS itself is known as a "chronic, manageable illness." You're more likely to see someone stricken with telltale AIDS symptoms in a museum or a documentary than you are on the street of any major city.

According to a study my doctor shared with me, there is little to no chance of someone with an undetectable viral load transmitting HIV to a negative partner taking the "pre-exposure prophylaxis" (or PrEP) of Truvada, a Viagra-blue oval tablet that combines tenovir disoproxil and emtricitabine. As those of us with less than 200 T-cells once took Bactrim to ward off pneumocystis carnii pneumonia, HIV-negative people take Truvada daily to keep from contracting the virus. Safe sex has gone from wearing a rubber to taking a pill. At least where AIDS is concerned. Other STDs continue to thrive.

To remain undetectable, I take four pills once a day: Merck's Isentress, a salmon-colored oval containing

434.4 milligrams of raltegravir potassium, made in Switzerland and formulated in Singapore; Reyataz, a half-maroon, half-blue capsule stuffed with 300 milligrams of atazanavir sulfate created by the Princeton, New Jersey-based Bristol-Meyers Squibb Company; Viread, an oblong sky blue tablet with 300 milligrams of tenofovir disoproxil fumarate, manufactured in Canada for Gilead Sciences of Foster City, California; and Norvir, a white tablet containing 100 milligrams of ritonavir, produced in Italy for an Abbott Labs spin-off called AbbVie Inc., located to the north of Chicago, a few minutes from where I grew up.

Since that winter on the 7th floor I've had a number of aphthous ulcers, easily diagnosed. I have had no reoccurrence of pneumonia and no close encounters with any other opportunistic infections. I'm so healthy these days that it's only when I cup my pills in my hand that I'm reminded that the virus exists within me. And will for the rest of my life.

My pills have allowed my immune system to recover, as evident in the 700 T–cells I average when I get my blood work done twice a year. My doctor seems more concerned with my cholesterol levels. Aside from getting older, taking the cocktail increases bad CL–levels. I've already lived longer than my father did because of my ever-present pills. If I came this far to go down because of high cholesterol, then it was meant to be, I guess.

Life is fickle. So is death. If I were in a hospital today I wouldn't have nearly as many visitors as I did back then.

In this era of social media, in which "going viral" is a good thing, I have fewer face-to-face friends and less contact with humans in general.

My 7th floor visitors sat by my bedside with gossip and games. They visited in snowstorms, on weekends, and off-hours. They slapped cold washcloths on my feverish head and pulled me from the abyss. Yet I see very few of them anymore.

Some have moved out of the city. Like Adriana. After completing her vet-tech degree at the age of 50, she now lives on a farm in upstate New York and rescues old horses, dried-up cows, and other injured and unwanted animals. She still plays the piano. On summer nights and on winter holidays, her neighbors gather around to listen to her and laugh.

A few years ago, she told Cedar Gottlieb to stop using her image, even though it's an icon of contemporary art, on museum walls and in private collections all over the world. As seen through the eyes of Cedar Gottlieb, Adriana's former identity will adorn posters and postcards and magnets and coffee cups long after she's gone.

I've held on to "Chiclet waiting for the profiteroles, Madrid" all this time. It hangs in my living room. I've been told I could get $20,000 for it. But I'm not selling.

Since the cocktail, I've lost more friends to crystal meth than I ever did from AIDS. I know plenty of guys who took their AIDS reprieves and turned to "Tina" and non-stop sex parties. Some of us can't handle a new lease on life. Most of us can't control our desires. And fear makes fools of us all.

My friend Andre—otherwise smart and healthy—continued to refuse Western medicine. He scoffed at the cocktail and Bactrim prophylaxis. He witnessed what I'd been through, and he knew the cocktail had made a number of us thrive. Yet he despised doctors, and unless taken recreationally, he couldn't stand to take pills.

He died from a case of PCP on the dwindling 7th floor in 1999, one of St. Vincent's last AIDS-related deaths. That year, the annual number of deaths reported from AIDS was fewer than 8,000.

Lung cancer took Kathleen two years ago. She was a brilliant artist who died before she got her due. One of her "hair pieces" hangs in my living room: a mobile made from locks of wig hair from the drag queens of boy bar and Pyramid.

My stepfather's long battle with illness ended last summer. My legally married husband and I visited him in the pale yellow institution in Wisconsin where he ended his days. We joked about getting a ladder and breaking him out of the joint. We reminisced about the summer trips we took as a family to visit National Parks. Although he could barely get out of bed, we embraced. It was as if an unspoken forgiveness passed between us as my mother's sobs sounded in the corner like Sanctus bells. His funeral was on my 48th birthday.

My mother visited my husband and I this past June, the week before Gay Pride. She can't get around much these days, so we spent a day watching tv together as we had so many years ago. Flipping through Hulu, we came across a network sitcom called *The Real O'Neals*, about a Catholic family dealing with divorce and a precocious gay child. We watched an episode together and laughed awkwardly. Soon enough, she was choking back tears. I excused myself from the room. It felt like some sort of progress.

Television has certainly come a long way since the days of shameful gay characters like Jody Dallas (played by Billy Crystal) on *Soap*. The gist of Jody's character was that he loved a closeted football quarterback so much he was willing to live his life as a woman for him. *Soap* was banned by the Chicago Archdiocese weekly *Catholic Reader*. We watched it anyway.

We also watched Sidney Lumet's *Dog Day Afternoon* when it premiered at prime time. I remember being confused because the network censors excised the "adult themes," without which the motivation behind Al Pacino's character to rob a bank, that is, to get a sex change for the man he loved, made no sense whatsoever.

These days, undergoing sexual reassignment for your partner is no longer considered a healthy course for a gay relationship. I like to think that we've come far enough along to know the difference between sexuality (who you go to sleep with) and gender (who you got to sleep as).

More recently I got word that Joey, who visited me that fateful New Year's Eve of 1996, was in the hospital with lymphoma.

I visited her at Beth Israel Hospital, another of the

ground zero hospitals during the plague years, directly east of St. Vincent's. Like its long-gone Catholic sister, Beth Israel is on its way to become luxury housing as well.

Joey looked beautiful, but ravaged. She reclined in a misbehaving hospital gown, listless and bemused, her pale skin mapped with blue veins, her hair in a turban to hide the "chemo clumps." I wanted to tell her she had finally achieved Marilyn Monroe's look—if Marilyn had lived to be an octogenarian.

It was satisfying to bring Joey Big Macs and the *New York Post* and listen to her fabulous stories all over again. After some vicious chemo and the loss of her precious hair, she survives. I would have expected nothing less.

My mom was always on me as a kid to finish what I started: Boy Scouts, baseball, football, all the things I didn't want to begin in the first place but was required to do because that's what a red-blooded white boy from the suburbs did. Coming from the mouth of a divorced woman, this admonition carried little weight.

At this point in my life, I'm wise enough to accept that some people just can't finish things. Joey is guilty of that. I'm another. I couldn't even follow through on a simple thing like dying from AIDS. But now it appears as if I'll get the chance to live out the remainder of my days on my own terms.

Recently, Alzheimer's disease replaced AIDS on the list of New York City's top ten causes of death. If my immune system continues to respond to my daily medications and the levels of HIV in my body remain undetectable, I may live long enough to forget that St. Vincent's, our grim Brigadoon of the AIDS Crisis, ever existed.

ACKNOWLEDGEMENTS

Many thanks (and much love) to the following, without whose assistance and/or existence, neither I, nor this book, would be complete:

The 7th floor staff at St. Vincent's Hospital, the indispensable New York Public Library, Klee Van Meter, Dick Eubanks, GVV, Matlock, Wendy Zumpano, Susan Bell, Pam Hoffman, Andrea Barrick, Erika Doukas, Stephen Dillon, Kathleen White, Gwen Engelhard, Kevin McHugh, Sally Graham, David Dalrymple, Magda Stull, James Vance, Dominic King, Eric Sanchez, Jillian Blume, Gregg Hubbard, Andrea Smith, Carlton Jones, Pia Guccione, Peter Benassi, JoJo Americo, Connie Fleming, Arielle Fox, Christina Fragola, Penny Hanin, Paulo Santos, Mike Iveson, Annie Iobst, Aaron Andre, Sulyn Silbar, Lucy Sexton, Darinka Chase, Claudia Cuseta, Robin Peña, Rosa Bravo, Bruce Fuller, Keith Cokes, Rick Colon, Larry Goldhuber, Joey Gabriel, International Chrysis, Sister Virginine, Mrs. Johnson, Andrew Zerman, Christopher Bram, Raven-O, the queens from boy bar and Pyramid, and the ghosts of St. Vincent's.

RESOURCES

Most of the factual information and much of the inspiration that form the backbone of this book were provided by the following:

Savage Beauty, Nancy Milford (2001, Random House)

The Selected Poetry of Edna St. Vincent Millay, Nancy Milford, editor (2002, Modern Library Classics)

A History of St. Vincent's Hospital in New York City, George R. Stuart (1938, Alumnae Association of St. Vincent's Hospital School of Nursing)

It Seemed Important at the Time, Gloria Vanderbilt (2009, Simon & Schuster)

History of Medicine in New York: Three Centuries of Medical Progress, James J. Walsh & George Shrady, MD, (1919, National Americana Society, Inc.)

The Other Side of Silence: Men's Lives and Gay Identity—A Twentieth-Century History, John Lougherty (1998, Henry Holt & Co.)

J. Edgar Hoover: The Man and the Secrets, Curt Gentry (1991, WW Norton & Co, Inc.)

Stonewall: The Riots That Sparked the Gay Revolution, David Carter (2005, MacMillan)

I Slept with Joey Ramone: A Punk Rock Family Memoir, Mickey Leigh & Legs McNeil (2010, Simon and Schuster/Touchstone)

Hold Tight Gently: Michael Callen, Essex Hemphill and the Battlefield of AIDS, Martin Duberman (2014, The New Press)

The Things They Carried, Tim O'Brien (1990, Houghton Mifflin)

The Decline of the West, Oswald Spengler (1918)

Dancer From the Dance, Andrew Holleran (1978, William Morrow & Co.)

Our Lady of the Flowers (1943) and *Thieves' Journal,* Jean Genet (1949)

Voices in the Band, Susan C. Ball, (2015, Cornell University Press)

And the Band Played On, Randy Shilts (1987, St. Martin's Press)

The AIDS Generation: Stories of Survival and Resistance, Peter Halkitis (2014, Oxford University Press)

The Black Riders and Other Lines, Stephen Crane (1895, Copeland & Day)

Just Kids, Patti Smith (2010, ecco)

Mapplethorpe: A Biography, Patricia Morrisroe (1995, Random House)

Wagstaff: Before and After Mapplethorpe, Philip Gefter (2014, Liveright)

The Celluloid Closet (Revised Edition), Vito Russo (1987, Harper & Row)

A Grief Observed, C.S. Lewis (1961, Faber & Faber)

Vito: The Life of Gay Activist Vito Russo, Jeffrey Schwarz (July 23, 2013, HBO Documentary Productions)

The Normal Heart by Larry Kramer, premiered at The Public Theater, April 21, 1985

"Where St. Vincent's Once Stood," C. J. Hughes, *The New York Times,* October 25, 2013

"RIP St. Vincent's Hospital," Tom Robbins, *Village Voice,* April 13, 2010

"DA eyes St. Vinny's 'go-for-broke plan'", *NY Post,* August 21, 2011

"Remembering St. Vincent's," Andrew Boynton, *The New Yorker,* May 17, 2013

"Another Kind of AIDS Crisis," David France, *New York,* November 9, 2009

"Reagan's Legacy," Hank Plante, San Francisco Aids Foundation website, February, 2011

"The President's News Conference, September 17, 1985," Reagan Library Archives online

"Sidney Lumet—The Little Kid Actor Who Grew Up To Be a Bog-Time Director," Guy Flatley, *Moviecrazed* website, from a 1974 interview

"The Boys in the Snake Pit: Games 'Straights' Play," Jonathan Black, *Village Voice,* March 19, 1970

"Ten Things About Joey Ramone," Mayer Nissim, *Digital Spy* website, April 15, 2011

"A Ship-like Building Gets Another New Life," David W. Dunlap, *The New York Times,* December 5, 2013

"The Lost Sheridan Theater—7th Avenue and West 12th Street," Tom Miller, *Daytonian in Manhattan* website, January 25, 2016

"In an Excruciatingly Hip Neighborhood a Bloody Encounter," Michael Wilson, *The New York Times,* April 11, 2014

"Robert Mapplethorpe's Proud Finale," Dominick Dunne, *Vanity Fair,* February, 1989

"ZERO: no linked HIV transmissions in PARTNER study after couples had sex 58,000 times without condoms," Simon Collins, i-base.info, August 1, 2016.

"Alzheimer's, A Neglected Epidemic," Ginia Bellafante, *The New York Times,* May 18, 2014

And various stories from the September 19, 1921, November 14, 1935, June 17, 1957, and March 18, 1986 issues of *The New York Times.*

Tom Eubanks lives in Upstate Manhattan.
GHOSTS OF ST. VINCENT'S is not his first book.
He hopes it's not his last.

Visit www.ghostsofstvincents.com

or

follow @tomusphere on Twitter and/or Instagram.

22504632R00130

Printed in Great Britain
by Amazon